PORTUGUESE WOMEN'S WRITING
1972 TO 1986

PORTUGUESE WOMEN'S WRITING
1972 TO 1986
Reincarnations of a Revolution

Hilary Owen

Women's Studies
Volume 29

The Edwin Mellen Press
Lewiston•Queenston•Lampeter

Library of Congress Cataloging-in-Publication Data

Owen, Hilary, 1961-
    Portuguese women's writing : 1972 to 1986 / Hilary Owen.
        p. cm. -- (Women's studies ; v. 29)
    Includes bibliographical references and index.
    ISBN 0-7734-7517-6
    1. Portuguese fiction--Women authors--History and criticism. 2. Portuguese
fiction--20th century--History and criticism. 3. Portugal--History--Revolution,
1974--Literature and the revolution. I. Title. II. Women's studies (Lewiston, N.Y.) ; v.
29.

PQ9033 .O84 2000
869.3'42099287--dc21

                                                                        00-052522

This is volume 29 in the continuing series
Women's Studies
Volume 29 ISBN 0-7734-7517-6
WS Series ISBN 0-88946-118-X

A CIP catalog record for this book is available from the British Library.

        The Edwin Mellen Press   The Edwin Mellen Press
                Box 450   Box 67
        Lewiston, New York   Queenston, Ontario
        USA 14092-0450   CANADA L0S 1L0

                        The Edwin Mellen Press, Ltd.
                        Lampeter, Ceredigion, Wales
                        UNITED KINGDOM SA48 8LT

                Printed in the United States of America

For Mum, Dad and Till

Table of Contents

ABBREVIATIONS

MDM	Movimento Democrático de Mulheres
MLM	Movimento de Libertação das Mulheres
Notícia	*Notícia da Cidade Silvestre*
Novas Cartas	*Novas Cartas Portuguesas*
Paisagem	*Paisagem com Mulher e Mar ao Fundo*
PCP	Partido Comunista Português
PIDE	Polícia Internacional e de Defesa do Estado
PS	Partido Socialista

ACKNOWLEDGEMENTS

First and foremost, I am very much indebted to all of the writers in Portugal whose works form the principle focus of this volume. Maria Isabel Barreno, Maria Teresa Horta, Maria Velho da Costa, Teolinda Gersão, Hélia Correia, Olga Gonçalves and Lídia Jorge all gave generously of their time and knowledge in meetings and interviews back in the mid-1980s when this project first began as a PhD thesis. I am particularly grateful to Hélia and Rui for their practical and intellectual support over many years. In addition to the above, I would like to thank Helena Roseta, Maria de Lourdes Pintasilgo and Duarte Vidal for the valuable insights which their interviews afforded me. My appreciation is also due to the excellent library staff at the Comissão da Condição Feminina, now the Comissão para a Igualdade e para os direitos das Mulheres, in Lisbon and the Centro de Documentação 25 de Abril, in Coimbra both of which were indispensable sources of material.

In more recent times, I have come to value greatly the stimulating discussions on Portuguese women writers which I have enjoyed with Graça Abranches, Ana Paula Ferreira, Anna Klobucka, Paulo de Medeiros, Pat Odber de Baubeta, Cláudia Pazos Alonso and Manucha Lisboa. My particular thanks to Pat, Manucha and Paulo for kindly reading the manuscript of the book and for making useful suggestions. A special tribute is also due to Graça for the exemplary scholarship and personal courage which have been her trademark in pursuing feminist research over the years.

I thank my non-Lusitanist colleague, Margaret Littler, whose collaborative research into Portuguese influences on the work of Barbara Köhler was a real source of inspiration for the present book. I am also grateful to Lígia Silva and Isabel Almeida Vervaeck, the former for bringing such a refreshing perspective to Lídia Jorge, and the latter for being always willing, and able, to cope with my varied requests for information.

I would like to express my gratitude to Relógio d'Água and Caminho for permission to print citations from the works of Hélia Correia and Olga Gonçalves respectively. I would also like to acknowledge the financial assistance of Queen's University, Belfast in the early stages of this project. On the technical side, the finished product would not have been possible without the creative imagination and design flare of David Potts, the very considerable patience and professional expertise of Jonathan Nelson in compiling the index and the computer skills of Till Geiger in a multitude of capacities. I conclude, as always, with my warmest thanks to Till for his support on many levels, moral and intellectual, without which this book would certainly not have seen the light of day.

PREFACE
Dislocations

The Revolution of 25 April 1974 marks an important caesura in the history of modern Portugal which affects all areas of the cultural and political experience of the nation. It marks not just the break with the fascist past, but also the accelerated process of decolonization and a consequent forced reconceptualization of the country's positioning in Europe. Up to then writers were strongly constrained by repression and censorship which forced them to adopt varying forms of resistance. After 1974, and especially after the initial moments of euphoric rejoicing and subsequent disillusionment with the inevitable failures of utopian Left projects, writers in Portugal were really able to expand their voices and stylistic experiments. If Portuguese literature had previously never been poor or simply derivative, it transformed itself into one of the most vital contemporary literatures. One of the most important changes to come after 1974 was the establishment of a considerable number of women writers so that the Revolution, as could not be otherwise, also signalled an important shift in gender terms. Obviously there had been important women writers in Portugal before 1974. The names of Florbela Espanca, Irene Lisboa, and Agustina Bessa Luís, to mention only some of the most prominent, mark 20th century Portuguese literary history with as much force as that of any other writer. In the first decades of the century women had affirmed themselves, sometimes as vigorously as in any other society in Europe. Yet with the advent of the dictatorship in 1928 and the establishment of the "Estado Novo" women were not only relegated to a position of legal and political inferiority, their assignation of the domestic angel role precluded in effect their cultural development and expression and led apart from a few notable exceptions, to their almost complete invisibility.

Outside of Portugal such invisibility was only compounded by a general ignorance of Portuguese cultural achievements. In terms of literature, except for a handful of specialists, only Camões's 16th century epic, *The Lusiads*, was certain to enjoy some recognition and that mainly due to its acclaimed status with German and English romantics. A multitude of factors could be invoked to explain this state of affairs beginning with the absorption of Portugal for sixty years by Spain in the seventeenth century, continuing with a process of decadence and colonialist ineptitude. The winds of change that violently brought down the monarchy in 1910 soon yielded to the totalitarianism which would survive until 1974. Given Portugal's obstinate policies of isolationism neatly contained in the Salazarist formula of "proudly alone" it is no wonder that Portuguese literature would not become known outside of the country's borders. And even now all that an educated reader in Europe or the United States might perhaps recognize are the names of Eça de Queirós and Fernando Pessoa, to whom, at least after the attribution of the 1998 Nobel Prize, one should also add that of José Saramago. Between the country's marginalized political situation and the scarcity of translations in a global market for which accessibility readily means availability in English, the literature written by Portuguese women has in fact been under a double form of exclusion as Hilary Owen aptly remarks in her Introduction. As such the present volume not only reflects on the dislocations which generally characterize the writing of the authors studied, it constitutes in itself also an important dislocation, in its attempt to change the reception of Portuguese women writers in an anglophone context.

There are a number of perils to any such project, all of which the author has carefully avoided. Perhaps none is greater and more common than an idealization of the works studied or of the society from which they issue, which is all too often coupled with an assumed superiority of the critical eye able to survey the "foreign" culture better than anyone else. Instead, what the author achieves in this book is a coherent and systematic analysis of a number of important texts which does not avoid commenting on their paradoxes nor on their differences from each other, while still being able to formulate a number of key observations that clearly demonstrate that the authors in question share a large number of common concerns. Owen lucidly remarks on this in her conclusion as she notes that her project does risk homogenizing and essentializing the writers and their various texts. But that risk was worth taking. Not only does the present book avoid such pitfalls but, as a result of her comparisons, Owen goes quite beyond simply introducing the writers in question to a non-Portuguese audience. The points she advances contribute directly to current scholarship and will have to be taken into consideration by anyone studying contemporary Portuguese literature.

One of the key dislocations which Owen sees in this body of texts – all but one drawn from the 1980s – concerns the questioning of gender roles in general and within Portuguese society specifically. This is in itself a difficult issue inasmuch as the writers themselves openly reject being labelled as feminists even when their textual production would seem to leave no doubt as to this. Owen rigorously addresses these questions taking care to contextualize her analysis of the texts and noting the convoluted ways in which, though contesting patriarchy, the writers show strong political fissures among themselves. Indeed, the constant attention to the political issues related to the texts, and thus not only to textual politics but also in terms of policy, is one of the strong points of the present study. The ways in which Owen shows the writers' diverse engagements with the regulation of women's desire and related issues such as the idea of the family, abortion, and generational conflicts make this study of interest beyond strictly literary studies. Although one could certainly take issue with the choice of texts made by Owen as to why a certain novel is discussed and not another by the same author, it is useful to keep in mind that this is not a survey nor a simple introduction and that instead of a pretended coverage there is much more an attempt to illustrate certain points by focusing on a limited number of texts. In this light, Owen's strategy to initiate her discussion with an analysis of *The New*

Portuguese Letters, a seminal text of 1972 which both predates the revolution and adumbrates many of the precise issues that would intensely engage women writers in Portugal after that time, is another strong point. There is no desire, in so doing, to posit this collective text as in some way originary - the text's own textuality with its critique of origins would preclude such a view - nor to assemble some form of women's tradition even if some writers explicitly acknowledge their indebtedness to the three writers who, at the risk of their own imprisonment, openly defied the regime's repression. However, *The New Portuguese Letters*, by now seemingly forgotten by many, not only caused a scandal in Portugal at the time of its publication but, more importantly, could be considered at the forefront of feminist attempts to question patriarchy, the state, colonialism, and a division between men and women which reduced both to less than their potential. As such, that text could be seen as effecting an important dislocation of its own, annulling the dichotomy by which Portugal and its literature were seen as peripheral and imposing itself in theoretical terms as much as a work of literature. Starting her book with a discussion of this text Owen not only sets up the terms of her own discussion to ensue but also already points out the necessity of considering Portuguese women writers when discussing feminist issues.

Another important strategy of the present volume is the consistent and varied theoretical approach to the texts at issue. Not only does Owen thus facilitate an integration of these texts into other frames of study but also opens up novel perspectives. Thus, instead of relying on one single theoretical point of view, Owen has recourse to the insights afforded by Foucault and Braidotti, Lacan and Bhabha, Kristeva and Deleuze, to probe the texts from different locations. Rather than constituting an easy sell-out to theoretical pluralism, given the book's goal of providing access to the texts, such a decision assumes heuristic qualities: readers are shown a multiplicity of possible ways of analyzing the texts at the same time that they are encouraged to pursue their own and thus to integrate the texts into broader discussions. Also, and this is no small point, there is never any idealization of renowned, non-Portuguese, theoreticians. Even if

Deleuze's concept of the "minor" is adopted to look at the production of Portuguese women writers and specifically with reference to the work of Lídia Jorge – arguably one of Portugal's most important writers – the possible shortcomings of such a concept in reference to women are also demonstrated. Furthermore, Owen refers as much to Portuguese scholars and specialists in Portuguese literature as she does to more internationally recognized ones.

In the last fifteen years there has been a burgeoning of studies on both nationalism and postcolonialism, with practically no consideration of either Portuguese texts or historical circumstances. In this respect too the present study can be seen as making some impact. As Owen clearly demonstrates, one of the common links between the writers she focuses on is a reconsideration not only of Portugal as a nation but of the way in which gender plays a role in that process. And the novels demonstrate over and again that issues of colonization can never be avoided in such a project. Owen's focus on Hélia Correia's *Montedemo* and its clear exposition of the complexity of the issues of community, women's bodies, popular rites, and state and church repression, is paradigmatic. The young woman who seemingly inexplicably conceives a black child is ostracized by her rural community and, as Owen notes, "the maternal and colonial bodies, historically repressed under Salazarism, return only to be all the more violently re-repressed in the affirmation of more fundamental cultural taboo" (68). Power and desire, the materiality of bodies, post-revolutionary allegories, the construction and the engendering of the nation, as well as the way in which Portugal's colonial enterprise forcibly necessitates a consideration of Africa for any understanding of Portuguese society, are all points which recur in Owen's study. In a sense, beyond mapping female territories in contemporary Portuguese literature and making these more accessible to scholars and students outside of Portugal, this book also in fact charts some of the ways in which Portuguese Studies are inevitably developing.

Paulo de Medeiros
Universiteit Utrecht

INTRODUCTION

Women's Writing in Portugal: This feminism which is not one

In this book I aim to analyze six different works of narrative fiction written by women writers in late twentieth-century Portugal. I take as my starting point, *Novas Cartas Portuguesas,* published two years before the 25 April 1974 Revolution which brought Europe's longest dictatorship to an end. The theoretical issues which *Novas Cartas Portuguesas* raises about gender, sexual difference, and literary and political representation, provide a historically specific critical framework for my readings of women's texts from the post-revolutionary period.[1] I also undertake the necessary critical task of locating contemporary women's writing in Portugal in relation to the predominant Euro-American feminist theoretical debates of the 1970s and 1980s. The five post-1974 texts upon which I focus were produced between 1977 and 1986, the period which witnessed the end of Portugal's revolutionary crisis, its democratic transition, the continued after-effects of decolonization and preparation to enter the European Communities in 1986. The re-narrativization of these events in creative fiction, from variously realist and (post)modernist perspectives, forms a common context for all of the works I choose to study. For this reason, a brief historical exposition presents an essential, if somewhat conventional, starting point from which to explore the strategies women writers have adopted for countering the exclusion

---

[1] The term "re/presentation" will henceforth be used to refer to political and poetic representation, according to the *Vertretung/Darstellung* distinction which Gayatri Spivak explicates in her reading of Marx in "Can the Subaltern Speak?" (70-5).

of women's voices from the master narratives of twentieth-century Portuguese literature and history.

The Estado Novo dictatorship (1933-74) has been memorably described by Michael Harsgor as a "subdued Lusitanian Catholic version of a Fascist regime" (4) in his attempt to signal the specificities of Portuguese fascism in comparison with the paradigmatic fascist regimes of Germany and Italy.[2] The emergence of the Estado Novo parallels in large measure the rise of its undisputed architect, António Oliveira Salazar, who began his career as a financial law lecturer at Coimbra University, entering parliament in 1921. Salazar steadily gained a reputation for his powers of economic management and became Minister of Finance in 1928, following the 1926 military coup, which had brought the Portuguese Republic (1910-26) to an end. Carving out a niche of increasing power and influence in the context of the world economic crisis (1929-1933), he became Prime Minister in 1932. From this position he went on to formulate the Estado Novo regime of which he was supreme ruler from 1932 to 1968. The foundational act of this new political system was the Constitution of 1933. Partly inspired by Hitler and Mussolini, the Estado Novo took the form of an essentially corporatist, one-party dictatorship opposed to liberal democracy, and balancing church, monarchist, army and urban middle class interests (Birmingham 159). Although the regime pursued neither the systematically genocidal policies of Hitler nor the mass anti-Communist purges of Franco, political opposition was violently suppressed. The PIDE, the Gestapo-inspired secret police founded in 1945, became synonymous with a culture of spy

---

[2] The fascist credentials of the Estado Novo dictatorship have been considerably disputed by historians, particularly in comparison with the regimes of Hitler and Mussolini. See Gallagher and Birmingham for arguments against the use of the term. See Rabey for a Marxist analysis of the Estado Novo as a fascist state. See Costa Pinto 1992, for a comparative overview of the Estado Novo in relation to Italy and Germany, concluding that Salazarism was closer to the "authoritarian 'ideal-type'" (74). While detailed discussion is clearly beyond the scope of the present study it is worth noting that sexual politics, long recognized as a defining feature of German and Italian fascist ideology, has yet to be treated as a criterion of analysis in determining the Estado Novo's relationship to fascism.

networks, local informers and the inculcation of terror. Neglect of education, high illiteracy and the enforcement of censorship also fostered a climate of ignorance and depoliticization.

Foreign policy entered a significant new phase when the Colonial Act was passed in 1930 whilst Salazar was minister of the colonies. This newly-awakened interest in Portugal's African territories, which had been largely neglected for four centuries, responded mainly, in the first instance, to the need for new African markets for migrants and goods following the loss of American markets in the depression (Birmingham 164). The provisions of the Colonial Act increased nationalization of Portuguese economic interests in Africa in the face of foreign investments in the area (Alexandre 49). An image of Africa as a desirable destination for white settlers began to be propagated in Portugal and from the late 1940s onwards there was a notable rise in primarily working class migration to Angola and Mozambique. The 1951 revision to the Colonial Act saw the official coining of the euphemistic term "overseas provinces" of Portugal, reinforcing the concept of a single sovereign nation as a transcontinental union of territories. Rhetoric notwithstanding, forced native labour was a notorious reality on Angolan and Mozambican cotton plantations. Indigenous populations were not legally designated Portuguese citizens and the "safety valve" concept of "assimilação" was formulated to grant improved social status to a small minority of Africans on specific economic and educational conditions.

In the general post-war climate of national independence struggle and the ideological shift towards various modes of decolonization, Portuguese colonialism began to seem increasingly anachronistic and became subject to international pressure. Having remained neutral in World War II, Portugal had entered NATO as a founding member in 1949 and subsequently joined the United Nations in 1955. It was in the context of the UN General Assembly that foreign opposition to Portugal's colonial policy developed into a major issue from the mid-1950s onwards (Teixeira 81). Salazar unwaveringly defended the integrity of the Portuguese empire despite growing international isolation, summarized in his much cited slogan that Portugal stood "orgulhosamente só". In 1961 the Indian invasion and subsequent independence of the Portuguese enclaves of Goa, Daman and Diu, marked a symbolic beginning to the violent overthrow of empire which would ensue on three different battle fronts in Angola (1961), Guinea Bissau and Cape Verde (1963) and Mozambique (1964).

If African colonial policy was an internationally visible cornerstone of the Estado Novo regime, the domestic oppression of women was rather less amenable to foreign scrutiny. The terms of the 1933 Constitution explicitly excluded women from legal citizenship under the Estado Novo on account of their "natural" sexual difference and for the good of the family. The notorious Addendum to Article 5 asserted that women not be afforded equal citizenship on account of "as diferenças resultantes da sua natureza e do bem da família" (Comissão para a Igualdade e para os Direitos das Mulheres 49).[3] The Estado Novo also reversed the various liberal reforms such as improved education for women and the legal right to divorce which Portuguese first wave feminists had managed to secure under the Republic.[4] As the sociologist Virgínia Ferreira has pointed out, the curtailment or annulment of previously recognized legal and social rights such as those gained during the Republic contradicts the Western vision of progress whereby "the establishment of legal rights and the creation of legal subjects are irreversible processes" (173). In addition to overturning these Republican-era advances, the Estado Novo adopted a number of specific measures to secure women's compliance with the Salazarist strictures of "Deus, Pátria, Família". The Secretariado Nacional de Informação (SNI) and the Secretariado Nacional de Propaganda (SNP) produced posters and booklets of rules on good household practice, although the use of oral propaganda such as

---

[3] In 1991 the Comissão para a Igualdade e para os Direitos das Mulheres succeeded the Comissão da Condição Feminina set up in 1975. References to publications by this government body will henceforth be abbreviated to Comissão.

[4] For accounts of Republican feminism and the unsuccessful suffrage campaigns of the period see Tavares da Silva, Abranches 1998b and V. Ferreira. See also the historical appendix in Sadlier and Glória Fernandes's Introduction to Pazos Alonso with Fernandes 1996, for good general surveys in English of women's status under the Estado Novo and the changes wrought by the revolution.

speeches and radio broadcasts was probably more significant since illiteracy rates were high (*Opção* 51-4; Baptista 191-2).

Studies of the popular propagation of Estado Novo ideology have argued that the Salazarist image of a thriftily run state economy without borrowing or credit afforded a significant discursive connection between the model Portuguese family budget and the operations of the state (*Opção* 51-4; Belo et al. 266-7). This, in turn, granted an illusory rhetorical status to the housewife, controlling the purse strings, in dutiful emulation of Salazar's "household" economy of the nation. The only national organizations to which women could legally belong were the Obra das Mães para a Educação Nacional (OMEN) founded in 1937 and devoted to domestic issues and the female branch of the Moçidade Portuguesa established in emulation of the Hitler Youth Movement in 1938. The closest approximation to a feminist organization at that time was the Conselho Nacional das Mulheres Portuguesas, founded under the Republic in 1914. It was forcibly disbanded in 1948 following a women's book exhibition in Lisbon. Its leader, Maria Lamas, was subsequently persecuted and driven into exile in France in 1962. Lamas's ground-breaking study, *As Mulheres do meu País*, published in 1948 was a moving tribute to the voiceless many who worked in rural and urban drudgery.

The 1940 Concordat between the Estado Novo and the Vatican made divorce impossible for couples married in the Catholic Church. Artificial contraception was prohibited and abortion was illegal and subject to up to eight years imprisonment (Ferreira, V. 173). The problem of illiteracy was particularly severe among women (Barbosa 477; Kaplan, G. 182) and the maternal and infant mortality rates were very high (Ferreira, V. 173). Normative images of sexual and social relations emphasized the natural complementarity of gender roles and the primacy of procreation as the only justification of the couple. The legal treatment of adultery effectively licensed men to murder adulterous wives, in so far as the maximum sentence for killing a wife under these circumstances was three months banishment from a man's home province (Barbosa 477). The absolute power of the male "chefe de família" to govern wives and children was further enshrined in the Código Civil of 1967 (Comissão 50).

This oppressive social context, combined with state censorship of newspapers and books, would not seem to offer a propitious environment for women writers to emerge as voices of dissidence in creative writing. Certainly, women who did write during this period were restricted primarily to the urban, educated middle classes, and their subsequent inclusion in the literary histories of the period has been selective and uneven. The emergence of the Marxist neorealist generation of male oppositional writers has, to date, been far more readily defined and territorialized than the contribution of women to anti-fascist literary resistance. However, Ana Paula Ferreira has argued with reference to well and less-studied women writers, that the 1930s and 1940s witnessed "the appearance for the first time in Portugal of a body of narrative work written by women and centred on Woman as a focus of ideological struggle" (1996, 134). From a Foucauldian perspective, Ferreira contends that both fascist and vestigial 19th century national sexual ideologies, harnessing localized micro-networks of power in existing family structures, variously constructed (and oppressed) women under the Estado Novo but also, by the same token, gave rise to specific discourses of resistance (1996, 138). My own attempt to locate women's rewritings of the Estado Novo period in the 1970s and 1980s, owes a significant debt to Ferreira's Foucauldian insights and also to one of her sources, a 1987 Lacanian study of Salazarist sexual ideology by Maria Belo, Ana Paula Alão and Iolanda Neves Cabral.

Belo et al. analyze the official propaganda discourses of Salazarist ideology in the light of Lacanian theories of subject formation and with reference to other psychoanalytical work on fascism, such as that of Italian feminist Maria-Antonietta Macciocchi. Positing the "feminization" of the Estado Novo, Belo et al. claim that Salazar's "feminine" or sexually ambivalent image allowed him a certain identification with the desexualized women his regime extolled (celibate intellectuals and repressed mothers), thus partly masking the naturalized sex differentiation which licensed women's oppression (275).[5] Although their study is inconclusive and limited in scope, Belo et al. take the useful step of reading Salazarist ideological discourses in Lacanian terms of the imaginary identifications of nation and state. Ferreira refines their psychoanalytical line into a more historically-located analysis of discursive power networks, effectively raising a further issue of significance to my study: the specific ideological relationship between differently marginalized groups. Ferreira goes on to explore the discursive link between the exclusion of women and that of other "naturally" proscribed groups such as colonials and ethnic "Others" which underpinned Salazarist constructions of white masculine national citizenship. As noted above, the 1933 constitution defined women on account of their natural sexual difference as the mainstay of the naturalized family unit which constituted both the basic cell of Salazarist society and the rhetorical trope of identification for the unity of colonially-extended Portuguese "nationhood". This concept of family as "a célula do corpo social" and "a primeira das sociedades naturais" (Baptista 194) placed it outside the philosophical purview of citizenship or rights, a proscription also extended to those manifesting "as [diferenças] impostas pela diversidade das circunstâncias ou pela natureza das cousas" (Ferreira, A.P. 137). On the basis of this Ferreira compellingly proceeds to argue that "the Estado Novo [...] generated a consensual fictional poetics of womanhood and femininity encompassing heterogeneous spaces and peoples characterized as 'naturally' different" (134). Diverse groups such as colonized peoples and ethnic "others" were thus bound by their "natural differences" into the unifying construct of the "greater national family" for which Woman acted as symbolic guarantor.

Ferreira affords a particularly valuable elucidation of the potential for connection between the diversely oppressed groups and materially distinct

---

[5] One problem with this is the failure to deal adequately with the dominant representation of Salazar as an ever vigilant father figure to the nation, albeit with a sexually ambivalent priestly aura. As Birmingham writes, "his propaganda machines presented him as a wise and monkish father, the saviour of the nation, pictured on posters with the crusader's sword in his hand or written into history books as the patriotic successor to the liberating hero of the nation, John IV of Braganza" (159).

categories of alterity to be found in narrative fiction by women which decentres white, male humanist identity and inscribes feminine subjectivity. This does not, of course, mean that the class, race and sexual politics of the period map neatly onto each other, as the current analysis will reveal. Nor did definitions of citizenship and their exclusions stay fixed during the whole Estado Novo period. Rather, the analysis of definitions in terms of discursive formations provides useful insights into the ideological context within which oppositional women of the 1960s and 1970s were still constrained to organize diversely and contingently in relation to both the Marxist class struggle and the decolonization question. It was this last issue which, for all that news in Portugal was censored and suppressed, came to dominate national life and intellectual opposition in the closing years of the Estado Novo.

The role of women in Portuguese society underwent visible changes as a result of the Colonial War, which had begun with the insurgency of the Angolan independence movement in 1961 and lasted until 1974. The actual, as opposed to rhetorical, families of the nation were increasingly diasporized by the military draft, the dodging of the draft and a rise in economic migration to Northern Europe. All of these had an effect on the lives of women shouldering new responsibilities in the home and/or finding new opportunities for paid work outside it.[6] As the anonymous author of "Salazar e as Mulheres" writes:

> A grande ruptura na posição da mulher na nossa sociedade só vem na sequência da guerra colonial, isto é, simultaneamente na sequência do maior desenvolvimento capitalista do país e da passagem forçada da mulher ao estatuto temporário de cabeça de casal. (*Opção* 54)

The incapacitation of Salazar in 1968 led to the succession of Marcelo Caetano who effectively continued in the Salazarist mould although hopes were briefly raised by the superficial liberalization programme of the "Primavera Marcelista".

---

[6] It also led to increased employment opportunities for women. As Virgínia Ferreira has pointed out, women's participation in the labour market grew significantly in the 1960s because "the male workforce was depleted by the colonial war and, above all, by strong emigration to other European countries" (165).

In 1971 an alteration to article 5 of the Constitution dropped the reference to women's special responsibility for "o bem da família" (Comissão 27) but retained the exclusion of women from citizenship on account of natural sexual difference. New currents of modernization and social progress were to enter the regime nonetheless through the experiences of migrants to Northern Europe, the 1960s increase in industrialization and the rise in foreign tourists visiting Portugal. The student revolts of 1962 and 1969 bore witness to high levels of student consciousness and mobilization (Abranches 1998a, 4) the 1969 movement being particularly influenced by May '68.

In this climate of anti-colonial and anti-fascist activism among students, writers and intellectuals the development of feminist movements in the United States and elsewhere in Europe began to have an impact among literate, educated women in Portugal. Graça Abranches writes:

> The narrow gaps opened in the regime by the so-called 'Marcelist Springtime' [...] allowed the impact of the second wave French, Italian and US feminisms to be felt in intellectual circles as attested by the number of books dealing with feminist issues published in Portugal in the years immediately before 1974 Revolution. (1998a, 5)[7]

These writers included the foundational North American thinkers, Betty Friedan and Kate Millett as well as the British Marxist feminist, Sheila Rowbotham. Proceedings of Coimbra student conferences on feminist issues were published in 1968 and 1969 and anthologies such as *Mulheres Contra Homens?* brought together translated articles and excerpts from radical US feminists such as Valerie Solanas and Ti-Grace Atkinson as well as the exiled Portuguese Maria Lamas and the more "canonical" figures referred to above. The predominant focus for women's organized resistance to the regime remained, however, the Communist and Socialist movements. Vladimir Lenin and Samora Machel, the Mozambican

---

[7] See Abranches 1998a, 5n for a useful list of work by Portuguese women activists in the context of Marxist resistance and papers from women students' initiatives and conferences as well as the classics of US and UK feminism published in Portuguese before 1974.

liberation leader, were the classic Marxist writers on women's role in revolutionary struggle (Kaufman and Klobucka 1997b, 16; Dionísio 501-9).[8]

Oppositional writers and journalists continued to wage their war on censorship, the most famous sexually motivated cases being provoked by Natália Correia's *Antologia de Poesia Portuguesa Satírica e Erótica* in 1966 and Maria Teresa Horta's auto-erotic anthology, *Minha Senhora de Mim* in 1971. By the 1970s censorship had become a rather tired ritual of attrition, resembling in Pimlott and Seaton's memorable phrase "a kind of animal dance in which both sides snapped and pecked with strangely predictable movements, but in which teeth and blood were seldom seen" (47). An indisputable exception to this, however, was the most famous literary prosecution of the 1970s, the banning in 1972 of *Novas Cartas Portuguesas* by Maria Isabel Barreno, Maria Teresa Horta and Maria Velho da Costa, who came to be known as the Three Marias. The book's three co-authors and their publisher were prosecuted under article 420 of the Código Penal on a charge of pornography and offending public morals. The book was the result of a collaborative writing project. A series of publishers initially rejected it, already aware of the risk it represented, until Natália Correia supported its publication by Estúdio Cor in 1972. The draconian response of the regime far exceeded expectations of the reaction it was likely to provoke.

Novas Cartas Portuguesas was essentially a series of letters, essays and poems which the three women exchanged at twice weekly meetings. They worked with the agreed rules that all texts would be written anonymously and no one writer could censor the others. The volume which emerged was a powerful denunciation of the repressive sexual politics of the regime, with several veiled but decipherable references to the national catastrophe of the Colonial War. A scandalous best seller as soon as it hit the shelves, the book continued to circulate clandestinely after it was banned. Anti-fascist support rallied around the writers on a limited scale nationally, and more prominent international solidarity campaigns emerged in the name of free speech, human rights, and international

---

[8] For testimonial and historical tributes to women's anti-fascist struggle in leftwing movements, see de Freitas, Nery Nobre de Melo and Organização das Mulheres Comunistas.

feminism, making a political impact through negative foreign exposure of the regime's activities.[9] Duarte Vidal, Barreno's counsel for the defence, warned that this particular case would cause "grave ofensa e desprestígio para o nosso próprio país" (72). In Portugal, *Novas Cartas* became a focus for journalists and writers of the resistance, such as Augusto Abelaira, Natália Correia and Urbano Tavares Rodrigues, defending free speech and asserting the text's rightful place in the literary pantheon of the nation. Feminist movements elsewhere in Europe and in the Americas took up the cause, following Maria Isabel Barreno's appeal to Christiane Rochefort in Paris. The emphasis thus shifted to universal transnational oppression of woman under patriarchy and the call for defiance of "male-defined and patriarchally imposed false barriers. National Boundaries for one" (Morgan 1978, 205).

It is now generally accepted in Portugal that the sexual indecency charge against *Novas Cartas* was a pretext for suppressing the nationally sensitive issues it refers to, most notably the veiled Colonial War references.[10] However, the sexual and national readings clearly co-imply each other to a significant degree where a certain "discourse on Woman becomes the privileged *dispositif* of (Fascist) 'Portugueseness'" (Ferreira, A.P. 1996, 141). It was the African decolonization question which finally brought the Estado Novo to an end on 25 April 1974. The Caetano regime was peacefully overturned when a Marxist coup was staged by the Armed Forces Movement (MFA) made up of junior army officers who had become disillusioned and radicalized by their conditions of service fighting the insurgency in Africa. The Three Marias were officially pardoned in May 1974. Their legendary courtroom solidarity gave way to a public quarrel in the press between Velho da Costa, who allied herself with Communism and the Portuguese Revolution, and the other two Marias, who also

---

[9] For further discussion of various aspects of the trial and solidarity campaigns see Gillespie, Kauffman, Klobucka 2000, Morgan 1978, Sadlier, Slover and Vidal. See also Owen 1989, 1995 and 1999b. See de Sousa 1998 for an interview with the Three Marias about the trial.

[10] See Guimarães for Barreno, Horta and Velho da Costa's own comments on this at the time of *Novas Cartas'* republication in 1998.

identified themselves explicitly as feminists. The exchange of published correspondence between Barreno and Velho da Costa provided an acrimonious postscript to the Three Marias' case, not least because both writers ironically prefaced their letters with the type of descriptive titles and modes of address which had characterized the playful, collaborative venture of *Novas Cartas*. Velho da Costa distanced herself from the international feminist campaign and the appropriation of the text by women's movements abroad.[11]

Barreno and Horta along with a small, diverse group of women, some of whom had experience of activism in French and Italian feminist campaigns (Ferreira, V. 182), founded the Portuguese women's liberation movement, the Movimento de Libertação das Mulheres (MLM) in 1974. This autonomous feminist group whose slogan was "não a revolução sem libertação das mulheres, não a libertação das mulheres sem revolução" (MLM manifesto), demanded abortion and contraception and opposed the oppressive structures of the nuclear family. It was criticized and denounced by the far larger Portuguese Communist Party women's movement, the Movimento Democrático de Mulheres or MDM (Mailer 219-20; Barbosa 478). The MLM's only organized public rally in Lisbon's Parque Eduardo VII in January 1975, was violently suppressed by hostile crowds and the movement collapsed soon after, though key members such as Maria Teresa Horta, remained publically active in the context of abortion campaigns. In their foreword to *ABORTO - Direito ao Nosso Corpo* in 1975, Célia Metrass, Helena de Sá Medeiros and Maria Teresa Horta describe themselves as "feministas revolucionárias" and explain how their original intention to write "não em nome individual mas em nome do Movimento [MLM]" had been overtaken by ideological schisms. It is significant in this context that post-revolutionary Portugal never witnessed the emergence of double militancy feminism, the dual allegiance to Marxist commitment and women's sexual liberation which had been a significant feature of the Italian and Spanish feminist second waves (Abranches 1998a, 6; Kaplan, G. 208).

---

[11] For a fuller account of this public disagreement see Slover.

During the two years after the 25 April coup, a series of provisional governments followed in rapid succession as a struggle for power unfolded between the Socialists, and the Communist hard-liners and radical left elements in the MFA. Vasco Gonçalves, a Communist MFA leader, was Prime Minister between July 1974 and September 1975. The period following March 1975 in particular marked the high point of Communist influence over the development of the revolutionary process. Banks, insurance companies and many industries were nationalized and the cooperativization of land in the Alentejo placed large estates under collective control. Middle-class intellectuals, writers and students with left-wing sympathies also took to the streets identifying with the popular struggles of radical social movements conducting strikes, factory occupations and housing demonstrations.

The political instrumentalization of literature in the service of the cultural revolution was a major theme of the 1st Congress of the Associação dos Escritores Portugueses in May 1975. Vasco Gonçalves's address to the conference declared, "sois vós, com o vosso trabalho criador, a vossa experiência, o vosso saber, que deveis indicar o caminho para a libertação da nossa Pátria. [...] Vós sereis uma força motora da revolução" (Dionísio 196). However, the popular support of the people never rallied *en masse* to consolidate the power of the PCP and the "verão quente" of 1975 saw an escalation of violent anti-Communist protests from the conservative north of the country in particular. The radical left interlude and the swing towards Eastern European-style State Socialism, were decisively blocked in November 1975 with the suppression of a left-wing military coup at a Lisbon airbase and the revolution ended in Tom Gallagher's memorable phrase with a "whimper, not a bang" (227).

The period of Communist and radical left ascendancy had a lasting significance for women in two particular respects worth mentioning here. For the first time in many decades women broke with their domestic confinement and engaged in public political activism, participating in industrial and agricultural unions, factory occupations and street demonstrations. Secondly, although the new Constitution was passed following the decisive victory of the Socialists over the Communists in the democratic assembly elections of 1976, the terms in which the Constitution was framed continued to reflect the radical leftist aims which had been predominant when it was drafted. The 1976 Constitution affirmed women's political and juridical equality, effecting a dramatic overnight change in women's status which Virgínia Ferreira has claimed was ultimately a mixed blessing for long-term feminist progress, in so far as rights were acquired "automatically" without the consciousness-raising phase of prolonged political struggle. This "granting of liberation" from above was not accompanied by the kind of changes in culture, society and state institutions which would be conducive to concrete progress in implementation and enactment. Boaventura de Sousa Santos has convincingly argued for the paralysis rather than collapse of the state apparatus during the revolutionary crisis of 1975. Using the term "parallel state", he describes how the compromise within and between military factions and political parties which resolved the November 1975 crisis led to "a constitutional state busily constructing a modern democratic capitalist society under a constitution that pointed toward a classless socialist society" (1997, 46). Partly as a corollary of this, women's issues were variously pursued in the post-revolutionary period under the conflicting agendas of equal rights and workers' rights (Ferreira, V. 175-6). The greatest ambiguities and contradictions, however, were probably those which surrounded the struggle for women's sexual autonomy.

Divorce and contraception were legalized very soon after the revolution in 1975 but abortion was not. Following the collapse of the MLM in 1975 abortion became a focus for disparate, contingent organization among different women's groups and movements (d'Arthuys 33-44). In the immediate wake of the revolution, the Communist Party and the MDM did not consider the abortion issue to be a priority and regarded birth control as a private, non-essential concern compared to the workers' struggle. An anonymous interviewer for the British revolutionary socialist journal, *Big Flame,* prophetically writes in 1975, "as long as deaths and illnesses from illegal abortions, with men physically preventing their wives using contraceptives, are regarded even on the left as a 'private affair', women will face enormous obstacles" (24). The Socialist Party did, however, support abortion rights as evidenced in their 1975 election campaign (d'Arthuys 90-93) and the prosecution of a prominent Socialist journalist, Maria Antónia Palla, for making a television programme on abortion was to become a significant focus for protest in 1979 (Morgan 1996a, 571). An abortion act was eventually passed in 1984 but allowed for abortion only in cases of rape, foetal abnormality or serious threat to maternal health (Kaplan, G. 188). Even these provisions remained largely inoperable in social practice, especially outside the urban centres. The abortion referendum of 28 June 1998 voted on the new, liberalized legislation proposed by the Socialist government and backed by the Communists. It was not successful but it drew too few voters for the small majority against it to be decisive, so the debate effectively continues as a new referendum is mooted at time of going to press. The continued struggle for full legalization of abortion has traditionally united women supporters in Portugal on strategically formed fronts across political parties, lobbies and women's groups (Ferreira, V. 182; Barbosa 480). A recent assessment of Portuguese women's activism by Maria José Magalhães has countered the classic assertion that Portugal never had an autonomous feminist movement by arguing that the 1980s groups campaigning for abortion could be defined as a feminist movement, albeit a contingent, coalitional one (cited in Abranches 1998a, 6).[1]

The early 1980s gradually witnessed the turn to the free-market economics, consumer capitalism and social modernization required for Portugal's entry into Europe in 1986. The Socialist terms of the 1976 Constitution were removed from the 1982 revision and the radical left assessed the concrete achievements of 25 April with a growing sense of disillusionment and regret. Writers were forced to rethink the politicization of literature which had dominated debate during the immediate post-revolutionary period (Kaufman and Klobucka 1997b, 17-20; Jorge 1986; Lourenço). The "intervenções" at the II Congresso dos Escritores Portugueses in 1982 indicate this shift particularly

---

[1] See Abranches 1998a and V. Ferreira 181-4 for summaries of the main parameters of debate regarding feminist movements in Portugal

sharply in comparison with those of the 1st Congress in 1975. The words of José Cardoso Pires, cited below at length, seem to symptomatize the self-questioning which his generation of anti-fascist writers underwent, as the commodification of literature replaced the instrumentalization of the previous decade.

> A expressão livre continua a ser uma razão do nosso quotidiano – sim, ele é a componente essencial do perfil que hoje nos distingue. Mas dia após dia a opinião social vai perdendo força, dia após dia o protesto vai sendo dirigido como uma rotina sem eco; e um enorme cansaço se apodera da colectividade afastando-a da intervenção e do empenhamento cultural para as urgências do sobreviver. Então interrogamo-nos em que medida pode a liberdade de expressão ser convertida num ornato ou num álibi de uma sociedade mercantil e em que medida ela pode vir a transformar-se num simples instrumento de surdos numa cultura massificada. Em que medida o livro? - perguntamos. (223)

During the 1980s a new generation of women writers emerged, four of whom constitute the principle focus of this study. All of them except Olga Gonçalves, the oldest of the four, began publishing in the early 1980s with Lídia Jorge's first novel appearing in 1980, followed by Teolinda Gersão and Hélia Correia in 1981. Gonçalves's first work, an award winning testimonial novel on Portuguese migrants to Germany, had appeared in 1975. As Darlene Sadlier points out in her 1989 study, "for the first time in history, there are at least as many women as men publishing literature in Portugal" (xiii). In this sudden "embarras de richesse" of narrative fiction by and about women, *Novas Cartas Portuguesas* came to be primarily regarded as a symbolic turning point for women's freedom of sexual expression. Beyond that it was little studied or discussed and indeed went out of print in Portugal for almost two decades, becoming what Abranches aptly termed a "text exiled in its own land" (1998b, 15), although it remained a popular work in translation for international feminist movements.[13] Maria de Lourdes Pintasilgo, Portugal's first woman Prime Minister in 1979, wrote a preface to the 1980 edition effectively reclaiming the

---

[13] There was no new edition of *Novas Cartas Portuguesas* between the Moraes edition of 1980 and the Dom Quixote reprint in 1998.

text for Portugal as she stated "também aqui as *Novas Cartas Portuguesas* são pioneiras" (26). Explicitly adding her own voice to those of the Three Marias, Pintasilgo tried to reorientate a sense of women's liberation beyond class politics and bourgeois or Marxist revolutions, pointing to the deeply-rooted cultural myths and symbols underpinning dominant ideological formulations:

> Para além da lei mesmo quando não é acusatória ou não encontra falta, há o apelo às forças mágicas. Ligada, desde tempos imemoriais, no inconsciente social, à natureza...a mulher é parte integrante dos últimos redutos que o homem ainda não (jamais?) assimilou a si. (22)

Women writers of this period were united principally by their rejection of the descriptive term feminist, as they countered the imposition of labels and typologies in the name of their new-found aesthetic freedoms (Correia 1996, 51-2). *Mulheres* magazine funded by the MDM and edited by Maria Teresa Horta for most of the 1980s provided a controversial forum for reviewing foreign feminist authors and theorists as well as work by Portuguese women. It pursued a fairly uniform line of literary critique broadly based on sexual-difference feminism and French theorists such as Hélène Cixous and Luce Irigaray whose works were available in Portugal and had a visible influence on Horta's poetry in the 1980s. The word "feminism" itself was commonly understood to mean radical separatism and was not adopted by the Communist MDM, which stressed its class allegiance over gender (Barbosa 480). In this increasingly post-ideology decade the terms "post-marxism" and "post-feminism" began to acquire greater currency (Pinto, J. 5-6).

Portugal's old imperialist constructions of national identity and global positioning changed dramatically with decolonization and the move to enter Europe in 1986. Boaventura de Sousa Santos has famously deployed Immanuel Wallerstein's world systems theory to describe Portugal as a "semiperipheral society", negotiating a new world position in relation to the European Union, whilst retaining certain specific social links with the former colonies of Lusophone Africa (Santos 1992, 104; 1997, 35). Preparation for EU membership also became the driving force for social change, providing a renewed impetus for the implementation of women's legal rights. An increase in educational contacts with other European university systems followed 1986 raising awareness of feminist literary criticism and women's studies in the humanities and social sciences and eventually influencing the limited introduction of women's studies courses to certain university curricula (Abranches 1998a). [14]

Graça Abranches has suggested that Portuguese women writers' "double marginality, as both women and Portuguese, their problematic relation both to a gendered public discourse and with the past (what it was and what it wasn't) have produced locations that are more interstitial and diasporic" (1998b, 2). A significant question underlying all of my readings concerns the location of the women writers discussed in relation to the double marginality to which Abranches refers and the emergence of Portuguese semi-peripherality articulated by de Sousa Santos. The simple formulation that these writers are white, educated and lead middle-class lives in Lisbon hides more complex hybridized histories, identifications and cultural reference points. All of the post-revolution writers discussed here have knowledge of other European languages and all except Hélia Correia spent a formative period of their lives outside Portugal, an experience which afforded a crucial "other perspective" on Estado Novo society. Teolinda Gersão (b. 1940) was originally from Coimbra and became a university lecturer in German. She studied at Tübingen and Berlin, teaching at the latter in the early 1970s. She writes of this experience:

> In Deutschland hatte ich plötzlich alle möglichen Bücher, alle Filme, alle Theaterveranstaltungen. Das war ein Gefühl der Befreiung. Damals ist mir das Ausmaß der portugiesischen Zensur samt ihrer fürchterlichen Folgen zum ersten Mal klargeworden. (Hasebrink 104)

---

[14] The 1990s have seen a rise in feminist research in the social sciences and to a lesser extent in the arts. Undergraduate courses in Estudos da Mulher Sobre as Mulheres and Estudos Feministas are now offered at the Universidade Aberta and Universidade de Coimbra respectively. See Abranches 1998a for an interesting account of the history of feminist studies at Coimbra.

In Germany I suddenly had access to all the books, all the
films, all the theatre productions I could possibly want. It was
a feeling of liberation. That was when the full extent of
Portuguese censorship and its awful consequences first became
clear to me. (my translation)

Olga Gonçalves (b. 1929) came from a wealthy family in colonial Angola and

during the 1960s she spent seven years in London where she studied at King's

College. She describes the London years as pivotal in her adult life:

Tudo mudou para mim. Nota que eu já era, então, divorciada,
era uma mulher de 30 anos quando lá cheguei, decidida a ver
tudo bem. E o que vi foi a cultura daquele país (e a incultura
do meu), e o lado cívico daquele povo, passando pela Arte nos
Museus, o bom teatro. (Graciete Besse 107)

Lídia Jorge (b. 1946) grew up in the rural Algarve, a world she famously evokes

in her first novel, *O Dia dos Prodígios*. In the late 1960s during the Colonial War

she spent several years in Mozambique as an army officer's wife, which was a

defining moment for her in a rather different sense from the cosmopolitan

liberation of Gersão and Gonçalves in Berlin and London. In a 1997 interview

Jorge writes:

Living in Africa was a decisive experience. Africa spread
before my very eyes the theatre of life. I'm referring to the end
of the sixties and the first half of the seventies. From the
position in which I found myself, I understood what it was to
oppress and to be oppressed, what it was to have a comfortable
life as well as to be alienated, what it was to be a guerrilla and
a soldier. (d'Orey 171)

Hélia Correia (b. 1949) in contrast, has not lived abroad for any prolonged period

of time although she did spend summers in Paris in the closing years of the

Estado Novo. Her unconventional youth and childhood in Mafra were a much

more powerful formative influence. As the daughter of a well-known Communist

father she grew up with the omnipresent threat of the PIDE secret police

discovering her family's activities. She writes of her resolutely non-Christian

radical background:

Houve ainda mulheres ideologicamente privilegiadas, como é
o meu caso, que por serem filhas de comunistas, de

revolucionários, de progressistas, escaparam a todo esse drama
educativo dominado pela dualidade catolicismo/machismo.
(Letria 5)

All the writers I discuss have, in different ways, worked within and
against the "double marginality" of nation and gender to which Abranches refers,
inscribing Portuguese women's experience into the narratives of the post-
revolutionary nation in newly articulated relations with the former colonies and
the rest of Europe. The present volume is my attempt to explore some of the
interstitial and diasporic locations they open up with a view to expanding the
critical material available in English on Portuguese women writers. My project is
inevitably selective in scope and does not claim to define a school or a canon
although common social and aesthetic concerns do afford points of contact
between them.

My first chapter focuses on *Novas Cartas Portuguesas* as a historical
"ponto de ruptura" for women's writing in Portugal, licensing the literary
formulation of new ideas on the embodied feminine within language and society
but also, crucially, providing a necessary critical reference point for the
subsequent reading of those ideas. Assuming the right to represent women in the
act of representing, *Novas Cartas* signalled that women had decisively entered
the business of redefining the intellectual and poetic codes. It is in this sense that
Novas Cartas marks a theoretical as well as a literary intervention. It is not,
therefore, my concern to read *Novas Cartas* as a direct source of influence or an
originary inspiration for women writers of the next decade, though doubtless it
was both for many, but rather to suggest ways in which new critical directions
can usefully be derived from it.

Five different texts, all of them prose fiction, form the basis for the
remaining four chapters on the post-revolutionary period. These are: Teolinda
Gersão's *Paisagem com Mulher e Mar ao Fundo* (1982), Hélia Correia's
Montedemo (1983), Olga Gonçalves's *Mandei-lhe uma Boca* (1977) and its
sequel *Sara* (1986) and Lídia Jorge's *Notícia da Cidade Silvestre* (1984). All of
these are feminine-focalized and deal with women's experiences in society and in
relation to Estado Novo and/or post-revolutionary history. *Paisagem com Mulher*

a Mar ao Fundo is, on one level, a testament to the visible and less visible forms taken by women's anti-fascist resistance. *Montedemo, Mandei-lhe uma Boca* and *Notícia da Cidade Silvestre* are all set in the immediate post-revolutionary period of the late 1970s and the latter two engage in different ways with the "desvio em relação à norma" (Pintasilgo 1986, 64). *Mandei-lhe uma Boca* looks at the divorce boom which followed the revocation of the Concordat in 1975 and the ensuing destabilization of family life, both actual and perceived. *Montedemo* is more difficult to locate precisely but its references to colonial *retornados* punctuate the illusion of a timeless, rural Portugal with the social effects of decolonization. *Notícia da Cidade Silvestre* covers the 1975-9 period, charting the conscious and unconscious transmutation of exhausted revolutionary idealism and the material effects of decolonization on the metropolis. *Sara* affords insights into the depoliticization and social disorientation of youth in the expanding economy and the post-ideology climate of the 1980s. Since *Mandei-lhe uma Boca* and *Sara* effectively measure the changes between 1977 and 1986 they are considered out of chronological order in relation to the Lídia Jorge text of 1984 discussed in my concluding chapter.

As part of the conditions on which they come to writing, all of the above writers interrogate the gendered representations of the dominant national mythologies which the Three Marias so seismically decentred in 1972.[15] Virgínia Ferreira has claimed that in the area of social science research on women "the Portuguese [...] participate in international debates by bearing witness to the peculiarities of the social situation in Portugal, and not by contributing original theoretical perspectives based on a study of those peculiarities" (187). Given that the eclosion of literature by women has been such a significant phenomenon of the post-revolutionary era, I would like to contend that this is one area in which Portuguese women have contributed some original perspectives both theoretical and creative. For this reason, the novels studied here may be productively read

---

[15] As Regina Louro wrote in 1983, "a 'diferença' fora a marca distintiva das *Novas Cartas Portuguesas,* livro de que a maioria das novas autoras se reconhece devedora" (26). See also Guimarães and Seixo.

with reference to the terms of Euro-American postmodern and poststructuralist feminist debates at the same time as they supplement, and destabilize the theoretical frameworks these debates provide.[16]

Novas Cartas explores the negotiation between political representation and poetic re-presentation which is the traditional domain of the committed writer.[17] Drawing comparisons with the feminist theories of Luce Irigaray and Adriana Cavarero, I argue that *Novas Cartas* uses strategies of satirical mimesis to displace the dominant gender mythologies of Portuguese epic nationhood in favour of alternative models of symbolic exchange allowing for new expressions of the (feminine) embodied subject. *Novas Cartas* thus performed the major task of breaking taboo on women's desire at the same time as it posited a new materialist consciousness of the body, rejecting the heroic death drive and the immortalizing epic, the dominant modes of national masculinity endorsed by the Colonial War. *Novas Cartas* ultimately moves towards the radical renegotiation of the heterosexual contract as a possible new base for society. Reflecting the structuralist influences of the 1960s, the symbolic exchange relations of poetic signification in the text never become wholly abstracted from symbolic exchange relations at the root of specific forms of social organization. All of the later women writers under discussion here take this fundamental line of enquiry in new directions proposing different forms of narrative negotiation between the anti-humanist liberation of representational poetics from monologic (Marxist) fixation and the discursive re-inscription in society of embodied subjectivities, sexually differentiated by history and culture.

In analyzing their attempts to work simultaneously inside and outside of gender, writing the women back into Woman, my readings also owe a debt to the

---

[16] The pioneering works of Isabel Allegro de Magalhães *O Tempo das Mulheres* published in 1987 and *O Sexo dos Textos* published in 1995 both mark comprehensive attempts to study Portuguese women's writing in continental philosophical and theoretical frameworks. The latter in particular broaches the question of how French Feminist theory might provide a useful critical optic and follows this through with comparative readings of female and male-authored texts.

[17] See note 1 above.

Foucauldian-inspired concept of "technologies of gender" explicated by Teresa de Lauretis.[18] All of the works studied respond in different ways to de Lauretis's suggestion of moving:

> Between the (represented) discursive space of the positions made available by hegemonic discourses and the space-off, the elsewhere, of those discourses: those other spaces both discursive and social that exist, since feminist practices have (re)constructed them, in the margins (or 'between the lines,' or 'against the grain') of hegemonic discourses and in the interstices of institutions, in counter-practices and new forms of community. (1989, 26)

Novas Cartas as feminist practice effectively constructs a "space-off", going beyond mere dialectics to what de Lauretis defines as a movement between spaces, producing "the tension of contradiction, multiplicity and heteronymy" (26). One of the areas of contradiction most evident in post-revolutionary fiction concerns form and genre, the hybrid combination of modernist and postmodernist aesthetics, structuralist and poststructuralist theoretical influences, and vestigial or ironic references to the testimonial and neo-realist narrative formats which bore witness to anti-fascist resistance and revolution. Ellen Sapega has pertinently remarked that Portugal is "an extremely contradictory and heterogeneous space where premodernity, modernity and postmodernity can easily coexist and often overlap" (1997, 183). As all of the novels show, women's experiences in the 1980s continued to be overwritten by the contradictions between political and juridical freedoms and deeply conservative cultural strictures against legalization of abortion, divorce and use of contraception. In this context, the new narratives of the post-revolution afforded women writers, among other things, a cover story within which to continue speaking their own "revolution that was not one" in and through the gaps in the micro-relations of social power opened by the decentring of historically specific patriarchal formations. The resulting "feminism which was not one" went on to

---

[18] See also Ana Paula Ferreira 1993 for a discussion of Euro-American feminist theories, including Teresa de Lauretis, as the introductory essay for a special edition of *Discursos* devoted to "Discursos Femininos" in Portuguese literature.

proliferate productively in literary discourse, with heteronomous new aesthetics allowing women as writers, as subjects, as poetically enfranchised bodies to speak their own truths in a polyphony of new accents.

CHAPTER 1

Novas Cartas Portuguesas: In Spite of Ulysses

A convinced libertarian – particularly a foreign one – could understandably disapprove of Salazar. But I doubt that Plato would have done so. (Acheson 628)[1]

Nós andámos pelo terreiro da separação. (Barreno et al. 308)

Chamaremos crianças/Às crianças, mulheres às mulheres e homens/Aos homens. Chamaremos um poeta para governo/Da cidade. (Barreno et al. 75)

Novas Cartas Portuguesas, collaboratively authored by Maria Isabel Barreno, Maria Teresa Horta and Maria Velho da Costa, took as its starting point the French epistolary text *Lettres Portugaises* which was first published anonymously in 1669. This set of five love letters addressed to a French cavalier, the Marquis de Chamilly, was supposedly written by a Portuguese nun, Soror Mariana Alcoforado, from her cell in the Immaculate Conception Convent in Beja. The theme of the lovelorn Portuguese nun has been extensively reworked in numerous literary versions in and beyond Portugal as well as engendering academic debate regarding the letters' authenticity and national ownership in the French canon or the Portuguese. The *Lettres Portugaises* are now generally

---

[1] This was the impression which Salazar made on Dean Acheson, the then US Secretary of State on the occasion of a private meeting in February 1952, at the time of a key NATO summit in Lisbon.

recognized by current scholarship to have been an elaborate fraudulent pastiche, originally composed not by the nun but by Gabriel-Joseph de Lavergne de Guilleragues who, posing as their editor, claimed to have found and translated the letters from Portuguese into French.[2] As Anna Klobucka has suggested in her study of the Mariana Alcoforado myth, the nun was chosen by the Three Marias not so much for her tragic love story as for the relationship between gender, signature and traditions of authorship which her critical history metafictionally enfolds (2000, 136-50).

In addition to challenging conventional ascriptions of authorship, authenticity and national canonicity, *Novas Cartas* also transgresses rules of literary genre as the American critic, Linda S. Kauffman, has pointed out.[3] Combining letters, essays, poems, testimonies, reports, dialogues and citations, *Novas Cartas* is a hybrid, multifaceted project which grew organically through the Marias' twice-weekly meetings and exchanges of work. The ostensibly unpromising story of the lacrimose, abandoned nun presented itself as the perfect candidate for ironic recuperation. In the hands of the Three Marias, Mariana Alcoforado becomes a pretext for debating the very terms and conditions of possibility upon which women, as disembodied subjects under Portuguese fascism, could come to creative and political expression. Kauffman astutely concludes that *Novas Cartas* is a "work of criticism as well as of fiction, one that intentionally subverts the conventions of scholarly discourse that so frequently nullify the female" (284).[4] Expanding on this, I read *Novas Cartas* as a new critical discourse on re/presentation, subjectivity and women's desire performing the function of defining feminism, in Teresa de Lauretis's terms, as a "horizon of possible meanings" at a given juncture in history (1988, 4)

[2] For discussion of the authorship debates surrounding *Lettres Portugaises* see Kauffman C3; and Klobucka 1993, 51-56 and 2000, C5.

[3] See de Medeiros for a reading of *Novas Cartas* as postmodern innovation on account of its play with polyphony, simulacra, resistance of genre and deconstruction of origins.

[4] Maria de Lourdes Pintasilgo similarly suggests in her 1980 preface that *Novas Cartas* "inscrevem-se na grande corrente – hoje imensa – da literatura feminina em que a relação da mulher à escrita é um dos grandes temas explícitos ou implícitos" (26).

Locating my reading of *Novas Cartas* at the cross-over of poststructuralist feminist and historical materialist positions, I draw on Luce Irigaray's *This Sex Which is Not One*, in particular her concepts of satirical mimesis and her re-reading of Marx in terms of patrilinear exchange systems.[5] On the subject of feminine embodiment as anti-epic, I make specific use of the Italian feminist philosopher, Adriana Cavarero, who further develops Irigaray's theories of strategic mimesis in pragmatic, materialist directions drawn from her experiences in Italian feminist and Communist politics. As I will show, her *In Spite of Plato* recuperates the marginal female figures of classical Greek philosophy, affording a particularly productive re-reading of Odyssean myth and epic. The *Novas Cartas* project begins similarly by engaging in a sustained exercise of satirical mimesis, reappropriating the sites of feminine exclusion from phallocentric humanist discourse, by exposing the mechanisms of this exclusion through ironic, performance (Irigaray 1985b, 76-7). Rosi Braidotti has aptly characterized this as the "practice of 'as if', of mimesis as a political and intellectual strategy based on the subversive potential of repetitions" (1994, 39). The Marias write "as if" Mariana Alcoforado were an authentic biographical entity, with a context, a history, descendants and a family. Decentering the (masculine) false neutral of western humanist epistemologies they thus perform the nun's desire and abandonment as a mode of ironic displacement.[6] Refusing both patriarchal authority and the maternal phallus they expose the absence of the female body

---

[5] *Novas Cartas* was, of course, published in 1972 before the major works of either Irigaray or Cavarero. Kauffman has suggested that the English translation of the text was misread by British and American critics in 1975 because, "no one thought to place *New Portuguese Letters* in the context of either structural, linguistic, or poststructural theories, despite the allusions of the authors themselves" (307). Kauffman herself moved significantly to redress this omission. On discussion of the reception of the English translation in the US, see also Owen 1989 and 1995.

[6] See Ramalho de Sousa Santos and Amaral who also read *Novas Cartas* "ao denunciarem, como Irigaray propunha mais ou menos pela mesma altura (Irigaray 1974, 1977), a estrutura sexuada, porém, supostamente neutra, do discurso patriarcal" (10).

and feminine desire from Portuguese national literature and history, engaging in a series of playful re-inscriptions which work across various levels.

The Marias' satire on Mariana's family relations effectively dismantles the patrilinear genealogy which is the underlying paradigm for dynastic national history. Their anonymous letters and verses are written from the subject positions of Mariana, her lover and various friends, relations, descendants and contemporary Portuguese "Marias" and "Anas" whom they invent. From the inventions of Mariana's descendants, partial homonyms, and contemporary updates, arise other revised myths and other women whose stories continue. The figures of Joana, Mariana's free-spirited friend who also has an affair with the cavalier, and of Mónica who is driven to insanity, are destined to recur transhistorically. The chronology of the events described in the letters works against the chronological dating of the letters themselves, thus resisting the unidirectionality of historical teleology. The letters trace a story both forwards, though Mariana's successive nieces, and backwards through the family history, which emerges in the letters as a series of implied scandals and secret revelations. Mariana is hated and resented by her mother because the latter has also had a passionate long-term affair of which Mariana is the illegitimate offspring, and therefore not really, genetically, an Alcoforado at all. As Mariana's descendant, Dona Maria Ana asks, "não será lógico que as mulheres utilizem sua descendência sem nome nem propriedade para perpetuar o escândalo e o inaceitável?" (151).

Mariana's confinement to the convent in order to provide a dowry for her sister, establishes an ostensible narrative of rivalry and distrust between mother, daughters and sisters in the same family. As Irigaray writes, "the exchange upon which patriarchal societies are based takes place exclusively among men. Women, signs, commodities and currency always pass from one man to another" (1985b, 192). Through her embittered exchanges with her own mother, Mariana refuses the phallic, maternal authority, which traditionally betrays the daughter in favour of redemption through the son. The Marias refuse their condition as "commodities" and intervene decisively in the patrilinear economy of "hom(m)o-sexual" exchange, in which women as surplus value are always and only traded in relation to, and as an power attribute of, men (Irigaray 1985b, 170-72; 192-7). The aunt-niece relation emerges as a philosophical, intellectual counter-heritage of writing, working against the continuity of dynasty as the aunts are childless, and the birthing legacy is refused through Mariana's abortion. As Klobucka claims, although synchronic and diachronic axes of sisterhood and motherhood structure the text according to what she terms, citing Helena Michie, "the grammar of the family" (2000, 144) it is the diagonal aunt-niece relation which bears the weight of "generational" continuity in the text. Taking Mariana's name, as what Klobucka has aptly termed the "index of an absence" (2000, 135) the Marias thus exploit the power of discontinuity over linearity in favour of ironic horizontal juxtaposition. The name Mariana evokes the mother-daughter relations, left unexplored in the western Christian symbolic, between the Virgin Mary and her mother Saint Ann. The Marias unmake the patriarchal authority of the "proper" name Alcoforado, asserting instead the improper name of Mariana in different combinations of Marias, Anas, Marianas and Ana Marias. The concept of "legacy" or bequest, central to the economy of dynastic succession, is playfully likened to children's plastic "lego bricks" which can be combined in any number of polyvalent directions (310).

A serious threat to patriarchal social order is posed by the "commodities" of the masculine sexual economy ceasing to be a *mirror of value of and for man*" (Irigaray 1985b, 177) and setting up commerce among themselves producing "exchanges without identifiable terms, without accounts, without end... Without additions and accumulations, one plus one, woman after woman...Without sequence or number" (Irigaray 1985b, 197). The Marias adopt and extend this subversive gesture beyond their own circle and that of Mariana by speaking in lyric address to the 12th century figure of Dona Tareja whose negative image in national mythology derives from her subversion of the ho(m)mo-sexual economy. Dona Tareja is described as a "garotinha preferida/de donzel do outro lado" (296). Born the illegitimate daughter of the King of Castile, Dona Tareja was married to Count Henry of Burgundy, bringing with her as marriage portion Portucalense, the lands which first became known as the territory of Portugal. She is traditionally defamed throughout Portuguese history precisely for perverting the course of dynasticism by attempting to rule Portucalense herself as queen on Henry's death. Her remarriage to a Galician count led her son, Dom Afonso Henriques, to fight and win a war against her thus effectively securing the ascendancy of Portugal's first royal dynasty, the House of Avis. In the Marias' rewriting of her story, Dona Tareja is no longer a treacherous woman carrying her father's dagger in her garter as the myths of "cantiga e invenção" insist, she is simply a girl exploited as a token of inter-dynastic exchange. The closing lines of the poem redeliver her to herself with the words: "que te seja leve o estar/e solto logo o sorriso/o azul dos dias dados/de bom grado/ e o olhar destapado/para dar" (296).

The patrilinear (sexual) economy past and present is systematically supplanted by tentative discourses of female friendship, rediscovery of the other woman, the aunt-niece connection and the Marias' reinvention of their functionally "orphaned" selves as mothers, daughters and sisters of each other. It in this context that the Marias enter the text as anonymous "selves/others" who take shape, as in psychoanalysis, through the dialogic process of transference and counter-transference, each alternately the mother and daughter of the others (Kauffman 286). Betrayed by mother and father, the Marias are left without lineage, rephrasing the gospel injunction, "amai-nos umas às outras como nós nos amamos órfãs do mesmo bem" (51). Unauthorized by patriarchal or matriarchal hierarchy, they invoke instead a world of horizontal equality, "porque 'nesta terra que Deus criou, nós somos todas iguais, e isto nos dá a coragem de fazer assim uma aventura!'" (51). The adventure on which they embark is the rediscovery of desire, each in relation to herself and the other, in extended intertextual dialogue with humanist and Marxist master discourses on the body.

The most specific example of this dialectic of female desire and Marxist class revolution is the set of choruses entitled "A freira sangrenta" (67-75). The voice of the nun in this section repeatedly asks "e o que faremos, Madre Abadessa, que faremos?" as she tries to possess both body and bread despite the masculine monopoly on both. Like Irigaray in "Women in the Market", the Three Marias weigh the relative values of the virgin, the mother and the prostitute in this economy, before adding their own images of the transgressive female lover and the feminist rebel as possible modes of escape. The virgin who is *"pure exchange value"* (Irigaray 1985b 186) becomes here the nun as discarded "corpo inútil [que] no Senhor foi votado" (67). The fertile body of the mother is a "pomar de primeira" (68) woman equated to the appropriation of nature as landed property and "[re]productive of children and of the labor force" (Irigaray 1985b, 185). The hiring of the prostitute's body, which Irigaray sees as combining *"usage that is exchanged. Usage that is not merely potential"* (1985b, 186) is also intimately connected in "A freira sangrenta" with the body of the woman worker at the mercy of "os senhores de trabalhadoras e prostitutas" (69). Marking a break with Marxism as sufficient by itself to liberate women, the Marias claim that regardless of the class system "das mulheres todos os homens/são senhores" (71). The only alternative is escape into their own desire which leaves them no home in the world and "de irmandade/só o convento" (73). The sexual revolution as overthrow of bourgeois kinship structures may serve the Marxist revolution only for their brothers to say, "'fizésteis os cidadãos/agora a cidade é nossa'" (74-5). The Marias therefore stake their own prior claim to any reterritorializations the nun's anarchic body may effect, as they move towards a provisional *tabula rasa*, a temporarily suspended space of play from which to re-enter discourse as sexually embodied subjects.

In common with most French poststructuralist feminism and with Adriana Cavarero, the Marias' approach to sexual embodiment and mortality rejects the separation of mind/spirit and body, or psyche and soma, which underpins western humanist metaphysics. As Cavarero explains, Platonic philosophy relegates the female, maternal body to the devalued status of pure physical matter or "soma" as opposed to the realm of mind and spirit or "psyche". As a result of this, "a separated and dematerialized embodiedness can more easily conceal its sexual connotation, always marked by difference. Hence the male gender can easily claim to be neutral and universal" (26). In *Novas Cartas*, the letter from Ana

Maria born in 1940 similarly describes a bifurcation of male and female destinies, leading to the cultural imposition on women alone of responsibility for the biological origins and fate of all humanity, as she writes:

> Depois que foram bifurcados, irremediavelmente, o destino do homem e mulher – mas quando, mas quando? - sobre a mulher veio cair, além de todas as angústias vivenciais e de todas as repressões sociais que são comuns ao homem e à mulher, sobre a mulher veio cair a angústia do seu destino biológico, feito drama seu e não mais experiência dramática da espécie, e veio cair a repressão de que esse seu destino biológico feito drama individual é instrumento (219).

The enclosure of the convent provides the optimal experimental setting for the Marias to unmask the false neutral by reclaiming embodied desire for the realm of the psyche. They thus explore "the love of other women while sheltered from men's imperious choices that put them in the position of rival commodities" (Irigaray 1985b, 33). However, the provisional suspension of time, which the play-space of their experiment entails cannot conversely be allowed to re-universalize them as inherently excluded from history, power and agency. As Irigaray asks in terms which closely echo *Novas Cartas*, "might not the renunciation of heterosexual pleasure correspond once again to that disconnection from power that is traditionally theirs? Would it not involve a new prison, a new cloister, built of their own accord?" (1985b, 32-3). The implication in both texts is that the heterosexual pact will eventually have to be renegotiated.

The Marias' affirmation of the auto-erotic feminine body works on one level to re-inscribe the body *per se* as a living, vital and non-sacrificial entity in the national symbolic of Portuguese literature and history, liberated from the teleology of reproduction and death. The Marias position women's autonomous desire by way of decentering the phallus in the sex-death equations of the Freudian economy.[7] In this sense, as a necessary condition of their own re-embodiment, they open space to consider the transformation of heterosexual

---

[7] My subsequent references to Freud draw specifically on "Beyond the Pleasure Principle" and "The Ego and the Id" both reprinted in *On Metapsychology: The Theory of Psychoanalysis*.

relations, calling on men to reconceptualize their relationship to their creativity, as well as on women to rethink their relationship to mortality. Women's refusal to remain complicit with sexually passive roles such as "repouso do guerreiro" (218) threatens to disrupt the sexual economy of warfare. However, in its repeated acts of satirical mimicry and its dialogic projections and interpellations of the masculine voice throughout literature and history, *Novas Cartas* maintains an open dialogue and a negotiation with men, not a definitive split. In the context of the Colonial War, the Marias' rejection of the connection between sexual passion and mortality, the classic Eros/Thanatos pairing of Freud, effectively exhorts man to reinvent his sexuality as an urgent project to ensure his own survival.

The clearest example of this appeal to reconfigure desire and mortality is the suicide of Mariana's male cousin, José Maria Pereira Alcoforado. José Maria is deprived of Mariana's maternal affections when she is sent to the convent and he ultimately hangs himself from a fig tree near the family estate. The cryptic poem which he leaves as a suicide note, sounds the death knell of the "pátria" but also the death of empire as he writes "nem estrangeiro/nem menino/nem varões a assinalar/com o corpo de vosso primo/fazei Mariana um sino/que a Pátria possa dobrar" (171). The negative reference to "varões a assinalar" reverses, of course, the opening lines of *Os Lusíadas*, "as armas e os *barões* assinalados/Que, da Ocidental praia Lusitana,/Por mares nunca dantes navegados/Passaram ainda além da Taprobana" (71). The Colonial War, which the Camonian epic ideologically underwrites, has implicitly degenerated into a collective national suicide note. As Mariana remarks in her letter to Dom José Maria, he no longer dreams about the return of Dom Sebastião (167-70). His suicide is linked to his loss of belief in the mythical restoration of the Portuguese fatherland through the resurrection and return of the boy king Dom Sebastião whose death leading a doomed 16th century crusade to North Africa effectively brought the Avis dynasty to an end. The "bell" of Dom José Maria's body reverberates in the text through the contemporary figure named José Maria, a soldier in Africa. He describes to his friend António his fear of the war and the loss of his girlfriend

Joana, whose love of books and study is being encouraged by Dona Mariana
(190-1). Joana's refusal to act as a regenerative force for José Maria, preferring
instead the life of the intellect, emblematizes women's refusal to physically
sustain and replenish the cult of the absolute which has driven the nation to its
present extreme.

Where men can only depart or die, "bastava-vos morrer ou partir" (275)
and women no longer accept their passive side of the bargain, the future of the
country is deadlocked in a sexual stand-off which can only be broken by the
return of the men, but on what terms? The Marias say of themselves in
concluding *Novas Cartas* "nós andámos pelo terreiro da separação" (308),
pointing to the syntax of separation which structures the chain of epistolary and
poetic exchanges between partners and lovers across time and space. The myth of
Ulysses is recast not as the epic of departure but as the epistolary and lyric voices
of lovers' separation. Penelope is also satirically replayed through the endless
wives and girlfriends, commoners and queens, left to wait for the return of the
husband or lover, as soldier, sailor, exile or migrant, in the culmination of an
Odyssean adventure, which neither sex can continue to afford. Subverting the
myth of Penelope weaving and unweaving while she keeps suitors at bay and
remains faithful to Ulysses, one of the Marias declares, "mas em que teias
seremos, se preciso, as três, aranhas astuciosas fiando de nós mesmas nossa arte,
vantagem, nossa liberdade ou ordem" (42).

Adriana Cavarero's Penelope makes weaving the site of female self-
discovery, the "impenetrable space where she belongs to herself" (17) in response
to the Platonic disembodiment of the soul, constantly driven to escape the prison
of the body in the direction of transcendence and death. Her knowing and
subversive Penelope thus dislodges the Odyssean metaphysics of mortality in
which, she argues, "death defines its dominion in the wars, the sorrows, and the
fury of heroes. It is always present insofar as it is always challenged, functioning
as a measure of the challenger's excellence" (21). These unrepeatable moments
of heroic action must be preserved in the cultural memory in the form of epic,
offering the consolation of a kind of immortality against the terrifying void of

death as ultimate limit. Recasting the epic narrativization of mortality into the lyric forms of balladry, the Three Marias force new relations of symbolic exchange, addressing their heroic men *in absentia* or engaging them in dialogue. Graça Abranches has aptly remarked in this context, that the lack of genealogies and traditions of Portuguese women's writing has translated into a "closer intersextuality [...] with more marked re-accentuations, revaluings or underground interpellations of the alien masculine word, or into a more intimate dialogue with other literary traditions" (1998a, 2).

In the poem entitled "Senhora", the masculine and feminine voices alternate in dialogue. The unobtainable, cold and circumspect woman sends the man on an absurd quest telling him, "vai e traz-me um cabelo/dum dragão enamorado/Pois se me falas de amor/Quero vê-lo feito e provado" (26). She is told, in return, that her place is to embroider and spin, and not to know or to write, "não tem ciência nem prosa" (26). If it is his duty to go and "roubar o setestrelo/A um deus mau e zangado", it is hers to remain silently at home reproducing him in childbed, "deitada a sentir/Tua roda de fugir/Tua cabeça em meu ventre" (27). "Senhora" effectively delineates a Freudian concept of (epic) intercourse bound by the "challenge of an indefinite regeneration, of a reproduction of the *same* that defies death, in the procreation of the *son*" (Irigaray 1985a, 27). Running counter to this and exposing the epic quest as a near necrophiliac obsession, "Balada do Mal Real" shows the queen daring to confront the king with the spectacle of her own death. She lays bare the unequal costs and risks of the maritime enterprise to the king "que traz o mundo à cintura/e se deita do meu lado" (280). Sceptical of the power he derives from the conquest of the waves, the deathly blade which he takes for a defining limit, she tells him, "Senhor rei para manter-vos/não basta este gume de águas/este choro este receio/de pagar-vos só com mágoas" (280). The gifts the king brings her are fresh and living for him "de sol de riso e de arroz", but for her they are merely stained by his efforts, "o vestido que me dais/ de pena e suor de vós" (281). The queen's home, her life and her ability to love fade away with the years of waiting as she tells him "Senhor rei para amar-vos/não fora ermo o lugar/seriam fracos os braços/seria velho o falar" (281). He is finally enticed home only to find the queen has died paying the cost of his adventure, leaving him to tell the tale of his rebirth (also in Portuguese a pun on renaissance) from within the queen's skeletal bones. The queen concludes, "Senhor rei de sal e cedro/voltai vossa barca aos vossos/contai vossa renascença/pelo dentro dos meus ossos" (281).

Through their letters and essays the Marias disavow the amorous master narratives of western literature as inherently morbid depicting passion as a death drive which did no ultimate good to Romeo and Juliet, Tristan and Isolde, Abelard and Heloïse. In the exchange of correspondence between the nun and the cavalier as prototypical soldier, the death drive of Thanatos is always at work in the quest for adventure, locked in inseparable relation with Eros, the conquest of the body of woman. The Marias identify man's fear of "um corpo demasiado próximo da natureza" (91) as the age-old pretext for dominating the female body, echoing Irigaray's assertion that "man will be sure as far as possible of achieving mastery, subjugation, by triumphing over the anguish (of death) through intercourse…" (1985a, 27). The thrill of danger in destroying the nun's honour is a tame and cowardly version of the great death-defying adventure, the "diversão de mar alto" (32). Supposedly risking the excitement of the high seas, the cavalier never leaves the safe harbour of his own protective world and his companions. Mariana complains:

> É costume nos homens ser seu horizonte de absoluto o jogar com a vida da mulher, mas jogo sem risco aceite, senhor, como jogam as crianças com os sapos, que quando o bicho morre nem é pela mão da criança, é com seu espanto e mesmo com sua ofensa ao bicho que se morre assim. (134)

Where the horizon of the absolute is mapped onto the body of woman the cavalier finds only "le tombeau de ma présence" as he writes of the nun's promise to love him beyond death, "c'est contre cet anéantissement que j'ai essayé de creuser dans vos entrailles un abri" (97). The risk of death is, in any event, conveniently transferred in far greater proportion to the woman where the illicit love affair transgresses the Latin honour code in which the death of the woman must pay for the family honour vested in her vagina (264). Nowhere within the cavalier's military discourse of courage is there recognition of women's physical risks since "sangue de aborto não é sangue vertido pelo rei, é sempre vertido contra vós todos" (134).

The correspondence between Mariana and the cavalier also affords a series of subtextual resonances with the ongoing Colonial War, as it explores the sexual politics of nationhood and military honour taking up the theme introduced with Dom José Maria Pereira Alcoforado. The French cavalier has come to Portugal with Cardinal Richelieu's troops to assist the Portuguese in their War of Independence against Spain (1640-68). He is scornful of the Alentejan peasantry who he has come to save, and the sexual antagonism between the cavalier and Mariana is expressed in terms of French national superiority, the border being linguistically "performed" in a series of strategic code-switches between the Portuguese and French languages (94-8; 130-35). Where the French cavalier is the macho "colonial" exploiter of Portugal who identifies Mariana with her fellow oppressed Alentejans, "negras à contraluz do sol-pôr" (97) presenting an ironic and untameable "body" of rebellion, it takes little imagination to perceive the encoded analogy with the African war. The love affair with Mariana leaves the cavalier a weakened and sorry figure. He fears that he has lost for ever his military prestige, "meu lugar entre os meus, meu gosto de ajeitar-me bem à sela, à farda, ao bom comando, à leveza de rendas e casacas, à inteireza de servir com boa pólvora minha honra, meu Rei e meus haveres" (96).[8] In one of the passages selected by the censors of the text, the Marias take an even more obvious swipe at the death-defying, sexual posturing of a nation that fears collective impotence. They declaim in mock lament "ó meu Portugal de machos a enganar impotência, cobridores, garanhões, tão maus amantes, tão apressados na cama, só atentos a mostrar picha" (87). In order to save man from destroying himself one Maria imagines writing, but does not write a hypothetical letter to the man of the future.

---

[8] See Owen 1999c for a further development of this aspect of *Novas Cartas* in light of Homi Bhabha's theories on the dual strategies of discursive address implied in narrating the nation.

In it she stresses his need to be cured, a recurrent theme in *Novas Cartas*, of his morbidly destructive relationship to his own sexuality and creativity.

> (e pensei escrever a carta de amor ao homem que há-de vir a ser, lembram-se? É preciso curar o homem; dizer-lhe que nem o seu corpo é estéril, e nem só o falo é criador; dizer-lhe que nem sempre é preciso erigir para criar, e que criar primeiro para erigir depois pode deixar de ser um privilégio feminino. Muitas coisas, mas não se sabe ainda como dizê-las) (300-301).

This "dream of a common language" must strive towards non-oppositional embodiment, beyond the mutual trigger mechanisms of mortality and desire bringing men and women to a newly formulated acceptance of both. As the Marias state near the beginning of their project, "esta não é a casa da dualidade. Pobres, pobres os que são apenas dois" (108). In the non-phallic creativity which they imagine for both sexes the body is no longer a site of revenge against mortality. In the final passage, the unnamed "I" seeks her own somatic encounter with death, without endlessly rehearsing and pre-empting its limiting finitude through passion as risk. Hence she says, "Eis, meu amor a morte à qual tu afinal não pertences" (322). However, if man is not part of her death, nor is he totally excluded from the lived reality of a finite life, hence also the ambivalent double negative of the closing line, "não necessariamente meu amor sem ti a liberdade ou a pressa de morte no meu corpo" (322). Woman is mortal, so is man. Neither can escape their fate within the body of the other. It can only be shared.

Mariana's final letter to the cavalier, in which she asserts her mature identity as a respected writer, dismisses her love affair as a foolish youthful adventure. Mariana and the cavalier both ultimately turn back to the life of the soul and the mind. Ironically, what remains of their physical affair for her, are fond memories of him not in bed but in pensive mode, sharing moments of intellectual communication. She has used the experience to script herself as a worthy object of love. He is trapped without bodily passion in a dull conventional marriage and has lapsed into mediocrity and obscurity, neither killed nor liberated by the great passion he inspired. As Mariana remarks, "bastava-vos morrer ou partir" (275). He has never broken free of the compulsion to depart in search of a new adventure to postpone the fatal one. The final gift of thought and creativity is now hers not his. Not the immortality of the epic, but an acceptance of mortality and a revalidation of living matter inform the newly regenerated voice of intimacy, the epistle, the diary and the lyric, underwriting the possible vision of a new social symbolic at least momentarily at peace with itself.

The radical re-evaluation of heterosexual relations which *Novas Cartas* undertook along with the decisive installation of women writers as subjects of their own erotic and political discourse undoubtedly had a lasting effect on the next generation of women writers. This has recently been extensively recognized in the context of the new 1998 edition of *Novas Cartas* although individual writers, particularly Lídia Jorge, attested to the Three Marias' ground-breaking influence back in the 1980s.[9] Jorge encapsulated the feelings of many in a 1997 interview when she remarked:

> The *New Portuguese Letters* is about female desire. This was considered a crime in the seventies. Through the discourse itself, and the audacity of those amazing women writers, this book became a literary icon. It opened a way for us, which we have all more or less followed. (d'Orey 173)

In the chapters which follow I explore how women writers used the micro-spaces opened by this "ponto de ruptura" to inscribe a more confidently dissident feminine into the newly emerging narrativizations of the past. Faced with the disillusions and political compromises of the revolution, social transformation within stasis and the demise of an engendered imperial nationhood, I ask how women writers used the double-edged sword of representational language to speak to the "man of the future", when the future finally came.

---

[9] See Guimarães for the opinions of various women writers, journalists and public figures on the importance of *Novas Cartas* in 1998. See Louro 1983 for recognition of the Three Marias' influence on the new generation of women writers in the early 1980s and Pinto, J. for Jorge paying tribute to them in interview in 1985. See de Sousa 1998 for the Marias' self perceptions in this regard. See Horta 1982b and 1986 for commemorative tributes to the Three Marias published in *Mulheres* magazine in the 1980s.

CHAPTER 2

Through the Looking-Glass of History in Teolinda Gersão`s
Paisagem com Mulher e Mar ao Fundo

> Que mimetismos aceitámos? A que regra fatal do espelho nos
> sujeitámos? Que denúncias não realizámos nesse mimetismo?
> (Pintasilgo 1986, 64)

Teolinda Gersão's *Paisagem com mulher e mar ao fundo* (1982) is poised
between the past and the future, in the act of testimony which it declares in its
epigraph. Gersão asserts an extratextual frame of reference in the memory of
those who identify themselves in diverse ways within the collective experience of
oppression and resistance under the Estado Novo.

> O resto do texto também não é meu. De diversos modos foi
> dito, gritado, sonhado, vivido por muitas pessoas, e por isso o
> devolvo, apenas um pouco mais organizado debaixo desta capa
> de papel, a quem o reconheça como coisa sua.

The feminine focalization of the novel makes gendered memory and experience
the principle marker of diversity within this imagined act of collective self-
recognition and identification.[1] The novel's focus on polyphony and

---

[1] In press interviews given in the 1980s Gersão rejected the concept of "escrita
feminina" as a separatist aesthetic, a stance which brought her into conflict with Maria Teresa
Horta. See Horta's negative review of *Paisagem* in *Mulheres* 1982a. Gersão does, however,
afford significance to the specificity of women's historical experience and the material conditions

intersubjectivity is reminiscent of *Novas Cartas* and further emphasizes the differentiation of women's memories and experiences in relation to each other.[2] In this sense, *Paisagem* marks the impossibility of the totalizing testimonial voice at the same time as it recognizes the therapeutic role of a testimonially informed aesthetic, bearing witness to the past as a necessary healing fiction for the future.[3] As Robert J. C. Young has suggested in his comments on the political instrumentalization of psychoanalysis:

> Psychoanalysis covertly places the repetition of trauma within a linear or progressive model which is superimposed when psychoanalysis itself intervenes: the healing process enables the patient to break out of repetition. So the story that psychoanalysis really wants to tell is the saving of history from repetition and its transformation into the narrative of a successful case history. (145)

Gersão's own comments on the novel in a 1987 interview interestingly call for an allegorical reading whereby the mental breakdown and recovery of the central character Hortense represent the state of a whole society. She remarks that, rather than regarding the novel solely as a woman-centred text, "Hortenses Weg in die Depression sehe ich exemplarisch für die ganze Gesellschaft" (Prewo 18). ("I see Hortense's journey into depression as exemplary for the whole of society").

Gersão's Hortense is a woman artist who suffers a nervous breakdown and contemplates suicide when her only son Pedro is killed in the Colonial War.

under which women write. See her interviews with Regina Louro in 1983 and Inês Pedrosa in 1984.

[2] Isabel Allegro de Magalhães has usefully commented on this aspect of *Paisagem*:

> Se trata de uma voz plural, a destas mulheres, sendo o processo quase paralelo àquele que foi usado em *Novas Cartas Portuguesas*; aí eram as vozes das autoras, que se fundiam e confundiam, deixando dificilmente transparecer onde uma terminava para outra começar, como era aliás a sua expressa intenção. (1987, 449)

See also Ornelas for a sound analysis of the anti-epistemological destabilization of paternal law in Gersão's later work.

[3] Most reviewers of the novel in 1982 highlighted the significance of the feminine perspective. See Kong-Dumas, Prado Coelho, and de Magalhães 1987 for different views on how women come to voice in the context of the emerging resistant "povo".

Her husband Horácio has also died from the stress of working as an architect under the regime and being dismissed from his teaching post for non-conformity with state architectural planning. Hortense is left to find comfort in an uneasy relationship of mutual mistrust with her son's girlfriend Clara, who is expecting his child. Clara represents a source of rivalry for Hortense, but at the same time she reveals an obvious need for a solidarity that never quite materializes. Hortense finally regains a sense of personal subjectivity and/as political identity, when her initially disparate memories of youth and childhood under fascism cohere into a pattern of registering dissent against the regime. A new relationship with Gil, a *resistente* and former political prisoner, gives a focus to her previously diffuse and individual sense of resistance.

The psychoanalytical paradigm which structures the novel follows a Lacanian pattern of imaginary identification through literal and textual acts of mirroring, in which the phallically authorized entry into language intervenes as a literally masculine prerogative.[4] The loss of subjectivity is simulated poetically, in the first part of the novel in particular, by a paratactical flow of infinitive clauses without subject pronoun inflection. Hortense's name does not appear until page 38 and then only as she herself gradually remembers the names of others, Clara and Casimira, the family servant. Hortense contemplates suicide in terms of an act of non self-recognition in a glass pane, a "perder, de repente, a sua vida, e não reconhecer o seu rosto reflectido na vidraça" (9). Her survival can only proceed from inventing a new imagined unity out of the fragments.

> O real tinha-se tornado num jogo de transparências, ela era uma sombra num vidro...um corpo de vidro caindo de uma janela alta, um corpo rebentando em estilhaços de granada, para viver seria preciso recuperar-se, reunir os pedaços dispersos. (23)

---

[4] My analysis is indebted to the insights of Ana Paula Ferreira whose reading of *Paisagem* draws productively on Lacan, Zizek and the disruption of the law by the unsymbolizable "real" latent in women's small, daily acts of resistance (1997). See also Sandra Regina Goulart who reads *O Silêncio* and other texts by Gersão in light of Lacanian and French feminist theory and in comparison with Clarice Lispector and Virginia Woolf.

Hortense tries to communicate with Clara who works therapeutically in the manner of an imago, a projected maternal image-ideal. As a seemingly coherent and stable model for Hortense to emulate, Clara offers Hortense the possibility of a return to control over her sense of coordination, indicated by her inability to judge distances or differentiate herself from objects (Lacan 2-5). However, while Clara provides an external focus for (self-) recognition their actual encounters throughout the novel are characterized by silence or miscommunication, as the loss and reacquisition of language remain implicitly phallically determined. As Ana Paula Ferreira suggests, "it is not incidental that the death of her [Hortense's] son crystallizes the character's long-sedimented suspicion of how language mediates and authorizes the fictitious structure of the law [...] more precisely the 'right words' of Oliveira Salazar's law" (1997, 229).

The paternal law which authorizes the national family as language is symbolically instantiated by O.S., a transparent encrypting of Oliveira Salazar, but also possibly of "O Senhor" who is replicated in a series of dictators and patriarchs throughout the text. Hortense's battle with language becomes a quest for survival against the forces of O.S., metaphorized in the power of the waves, the maritime, colonial tradition which has killed her son and is now silencing her voice "para que só a voz dele existisse" (32). The tragedy of the Estado Novo and the Colonial War for women is the destruction of heterosexual love relations and of private, reproductive family life. Hortense's happy recollections of childhood festivals and family occasions are interrupted by nightmares of O. S. as a force of death and disruption establishing the recurrent flashback pattern of a trauma. Through a series of disjointed (auto)biographical micro-histories comparing herself to Elisa and Clara, Hortense begins to break this trauma of repetition by transferentially rediscovering herself in and through the other woman. Echoing the Three Marias' psychoanalytical process in *Novas Cartas*, where each at different times takes the role of mother/daughter to the other, the intersubjectivities of the three women are thus reproduced in a diachronically structured triptych of partial textual reflections.

The novel is divided into three formal sections. Part One corresponds primarily to Hortense's recent memories, the death of Pedro, her mental breakdown and her meetings with Clara. Part Two reproduces her meditations on painting and artistic representation, as well as her rebellious youth and childhood and her relationship with Elisa. Part Three refers to the beginning of Hortense's recovery and resistance through her relationship with Gil, just as Clara in contrast sinks into a morbid depression and takes up the first person persona in dialogue with Hortense.[5] Within and across the three sections, Hortense's subjectivity is reconstructed according to the diachronic temporality of the mirror phase as a movement of anticipation and retroaction. As Jane Gallop writes in her readings of Lacan, "the self is constituted through anticipating what it will become, and then this anticipatory model is used for gauging what was before" (81). The mirror stage thus follows the syntax of a future perfect, in the "formation of what *will have been* a rootstock" (81).

The future perfect structures Hortense's imaginary identification, however, in the self-conscious mode of a necessary fiction in that her projections of Clara are repeatedly shown to be illusions when viewed in retrospect. This is particularly evident in the calculatedly inexact mirroring process enacted between Parts One and Three as Clara's descent into depression in Part Three contradicts Hortense's idealized image of her in Part One as a self-confident survivor. The overlapping but non-identical feelings and experiences of Hortense and Clara lead them to misread and misremember each other in a downward spiral of solitude and disencounter. As Isabel Allegro de Magalhães points out, "talvez por causa do isolamento em que cada tentativa se faz: cada mulher, no texto, luta só [...] entre Clara e Hortense, há até uma ameaça mútua, em lugar de solidariedade" (1987, 453). The rivalry and antagonism between women militate against gender-based solidarity where "natural" sexual difference forging women in identical moulds is already the hegemonic discourse of the state. Underlying this, as *Novas Cartas* powerfully reveals, is the patriarchal economy of desire

---

[5] See de Magalhães 1987, 420-60 for a detailed analysis of women's partially overlapping life-cycles in the novel in terms of chronology and verb tenses.

casting women as competitors for men. The overlapping tragedies of Clara and
Hortense emphasize their acute need to join forces nonetheless, creating a
situational irony in the text left largely unresolved as a testimony to the near
impossibility of women's solidarity, trapped in the fantasy projections of a
fictitious state-sponsored femininity.

Hortense's private memories do, however, as part of their own conditions
of coming to voice, necessarily bring to light the experiences of the many
different kinds of women submerged within the homogeneous national identity
fiction she is trying to unmake. As in *Novas Cartas*, a panoply of diverse women
step out from behind the Salazarist sign "Woman". Thus Hortense's story
contains not only those of Clara and Elisa but her dutiful mother Helena, her
grandmother, the servant Casimira and the Salazarist schoolmistress, as well as
various anonymous cleaning women and self-sacrificial mothers, all of whom are
subject to similarly normative strictures regarding the home and the body. The
choice between complicity and resistance is written into the very fabric of their
daily lives where "cada coisa tinha a sua hora, a oração, os remédios, a leitura, a
rádio, o jornal" (85). The constant descriptions of Hortense's routines of domestic
feminine ritual environment, emphasize women's relationship to "nationhood" in
terms of what Homi K. Bhabha has termed "performative" time in his analyses of
the double movement of discursive address which characterizes the narration of
the nation. Performative time, as distinct from the "continuist, accumulative
temporality" of pedagogical time, is a "repetitious, recursive strategy" which
demonstrates "the living principle of the people as that continual process by
which national life is redeemed and signified as a repeating and reproductive
process" (Bhabha 1990, 297).

As part of this process of repetition and reproduction, Hortense describes
women's traditional complicity in the centuries-old national ritual of men going
to sea, as migrants, fishermen, sailors and most recently soldiers in the colonial
war whilst women, in the timeless pose of Penelope, stay behind and wait. She
imaginatively restages as anti-epic the famous scene on the docks at Restelo from
Canto IV of *Os Lusíadas*, in which wives and mothers bemoan the departure of

their menfolk to certain death on Vasco da Gama's voyage to India, while the men look away to strengthen their resolve. Remembering and renarrativizing Pedro's departure for his military service in Africa (46-7) Hortense realizes in retrospect that the passive fatalism and self-delusion of women in accepting the Penelope role are merely a pretext for their historical inactivity, exempting them from guilt and immobilizing their responsibility for resistance. Raging against the destruction of her son as extension of her own body and guarantor of her immorality, Hortense reacts against the entire Salazarist symbolization of the body as morbid, demanding sacrificial maternity on the part of women and sacrificial death at sea on the part of men. Her symbolic acts of displacement take the textual form of an active and dissident dis-membering which is also a re-membering, reassembling the shattered body in new shapes and formations, and producing a series of unsanctioned counter-discourses which satirically rewrite the national script.

This process takes the form of fissuring the imaginary identifications of the nation through satirical acts of mimicry and inexact repetition, recalling the strategies the Three Marias deployed in *Novas Cartas* although Gersão, freed from censorship, develops even more explicitly the imbrication of the sexual within the national (Bhabha 1985). Hortense begins to break out of the state role of grieving mother or "mãe agradecida" when she constructs an imagined conversation with a young pregnant woman whom she observes knitting and chatting in the sun. Listing all of the ways in which mothers protect and nurture children to adulthood, she points out the absurdity of keeping children alive only for them to die in a pointless war with national ideology inventing reasons to make an exception to the second commandment, "thou shalt not kill". Describing in mocking detail the care the state will take to tend the graves of its children but not their cradles, she parodies the official lies and blandishments of the regime offering mothers the compensation of medals in exchange for their sons' lives sacrificed to the glory of the "pátria". Hortense gaily minimizes the risk of death remarking "falo apenas de crianças, da morte dos filhos, é uma conversa à toa, um tema muito banal e sem importância" (54). However, where "a sagrada instituição do tricô" (55) distracts women from facing the truth, it is implied that the whole national order would unravel if women no longer found reason to knit.

In contrast to the passive mothers from whom Hortense distances herself, a potential new field of identification is presented in the unconsciously resisting acts of a series of housemaids, each unaware of the others and cleaning the separate windows of a large block of flats at the same time. Hortense describes "um quase humor na simultaneidade e na repetição dos movimentos, na perfeita similitude das janelas, nos braços segurando vassouras, com movimentos mecânicos, mas desencontrados" (30). Performing the same movement out of synchrony the women as a group disrupt the choreographed forms of the regime's activities. Further, when Hortense looks more closely through each window, she makes out a different scenario in each household. The structures of rebellion, however, are entirely in the aestheticizing eye of their relatively privileged beholder. Hortense as a bourgeois artist is not directly involved in the struggles of women as workers. As critics of Bhabha have pointed out, ironic mimicry and inexact repetition do not in themselves add up to political consciousness or material agency *per se* for the subjects who perform them as it were "intransitively" without an object.[6] In this respect *Paisagem,* like *Novas Cartas*, explores women's dilemmas of political agency and artistic expression as subjects of re/presentation whose private, sexual and domestic forms of oppression seem to be largely invisible to the dominant discourses of Marxist resistance.

As Hortense's case history shows, women's resistance could only find public expression as properly political through the masculine symbolic mediation of Marxism and movements on the left. Eduardo Prado Coelho's reading of the novel interestingly and symptomatically describes Hortense's salvation through political consciousness in terms of a masculine identification. He contrasts the infinity of the sea with "a finitude de uma Casa, onde a mulher, na perda do seu

---

[6] Bart Moore-Gilbert referring to the peasants' ostensible "misunderstandings" of the Bible, in Bhabha's "Signs Taken for Wonders" asks "is this kind of response a mode of resistance, and if so, is it then conscious or unconscious, transitive or intransitive?" (133).

ser feminino, encontra uma razão masculina de ser" (21). Hortense finally returns
to a sense of wholeness and sanity through her relationship with Gil, an anti-
fascist *resistente* who "a arrastara consigo e ela se abandonava em seu braços,
bruscamente chorando sem controle, e se deixava amar e o amava" (119). Gil
catalyzes Hortense's awareness of others as the precondition of her own
existence. She goes on to discard her morbid guilt at Pedro's death and celebrates
her return to life and wholeness through Gil. This act of love metaphorizes the
rebirth of a future with the restitution of linear time and historical progress
allegorized by the two lovers escaping a tidal wave of Salazarist lava petrifying
everything in its path. An orgasmic flow of vitality carries the couple to safety as
Hortense struggles to express, "este equilíbrio vertiginoso e cintilante, um rio
escuro, um sangue, uma cabeça, uma árvore num campo, inundada de esperma,
um corpo nascendo do meu corpo" (120). However, the same rhetorical
movement which brings Hortense to political consciousness and speech through
her encounter with Gil, also metaphorizes her as the traditionally silent maternal
body of the future, an image which is subsequently repositioned in somewhat
more ambivalent terms through Clara's reaction to her real impending maternity.

The male-authored mediation of Hortense's "recovery" from Salazarist
history effectively poses questions as to how she is to become the speaking
subject of her own history and how the real social experience of sexual
differentiation can be accounted for in the narrative of a resisting, unified "povo".
This question is most sharply focused in the relationship between Hortense and
Clara in Part Three. As Ana Paula Ferreira has pointed out, a major task of post-
revolutionary women writers was to transform and rewrite their role as
"traditionally silent wombs of history" (1997, 220). The celebrations surrounding
the "revolution" at the end of Part Two are juxtaposed with the image of Clara at
the beginning of Part Three. She is heavily pregnant and standing waiting in the
eternal mythical pose of Penelope leaning against the window of her flat.
Paisagem asks, as *Novas Cartas* does "qual a mudança, na vida das mulheres, ao
longo dos séculos" (152). It is Clara, not Hortense, who eventually attempts
suicide rather than face single parenthood under fascism and without Pedro.

Hortense's efforts to save Clara bring a resisting community to life through the anonymous city people who help Hortense in her rescue operation, organically represented in terms of the body with "o coração da cidade pulsando, somos um só corpo solidário" (146). The salt waters of the deadly sea are constructively reappropriated as the amniotic fluid of birth. Where the arrival of Clara's child allegorizes the reproduction of the "povo" as "corpo solidário", Woman continues to function as a rhetorical trope of unity for the community of the "people" much as she had previously done for the fascist family of the nation. Indeed, this link is prefigured here with the reunification of the diasporic Portuguese body not as "nation" but as "povo" with the end of empire and "o povo perdido pelo mundo reunindo os pedaços dispersos do seu corpo e voltando" (126). Hortense's desire to simultaneously "ser a mesma e ser outra" takes the form of "despir uma vida, um corpo" (122) recalling the self-renewal of an insect emerging from a chryallis, a neutral, organicist image of rebirth as a collectivity which echoes the common tropes of Neo-Realism. Women thus belong to the resisting "povo" only by neutralizing the historical and material marks of sexual differentiation. They are either elided into the body of the people, the proletariat as "une classe si immaculée, jusqu'à la rendre sans sexe, tout comme les anges (Macciocchi 27) or they are essentialized in maternalist metaphor as, to reiterate Ferreira's phrase, "the traditionally silent wombs of history" (220).

Where the question of sexual differentiation does emerge, it finds expression primarily through Hortense's youthful belief in the instrumentality of sexual revolution. Her relationships with her father, Horácio and Gil suggest that, retrospectively at least, she locates her powers of resistance in the overthrow of bourgeois patriarchy and Catholic repression within the family, recalling the theories of Marxist feminist Maria-Antonietta Macciocchi and her reworkings of Wilhelm Reich. According to Macciocchi, fascism and neo-fascism sustained by the spiritual authority which forbade abortion, divorce and contraception, "organisent la sexualité réactionnaire, non seulement de l'individu, mais de la femme, sous la forme de la famille autoritaire" (33). Hortense's rebellious childhood culminates in her leaving the family home to go and live with Horácio whom she has taken as a lover, explicitly defying paternal control. She recalls her military father "de pé em cima da pirâmide familiar, detentor dos bens e dono único da verdade e da força" (93). When she departs permanently she dissociates her own new awareness of the body, "vendo-se em corpo inteiro no espelho (96) from the specular wholeness which had only reflected her father. His phallic power is unmasked by the dissident feminine body which is "mais forte do que as armas e mais forte do que a sua lei […] a ordem que fora a dele estava quebrada, desfeita, o seu império em ruinas, como uma casa construída sobre areia" (104). However, the contingent instrumentality of the sexual revolution which Hortense implicitly invokes, does not liberate women from erotic or reproductive teleology as Clara's experience indicates and the Three Marias predict when they write, "*il n'y a pas de femmes libres, il'y a des femmes livrées aux hommes.* É essa a libertação que os homens nos oferecem, de repouso do guerreiro passamos a despojo de guerra" (218). Hortense's utopian focus on the dissident feminine body as privileged site of anti-fascist rebellion is subsequently undermined by the highly ambivalently "stagings" of the 25 April revolution which recur throughout *Paisagem*.

Nowhere in the novel is the revolution fixed as something that has definitively taken place. The scene which most directly approximates to the 25 April with its early morning radio broadcasts and carnations in the street turns into a dialogue exposing as myth the wholeness and unanimity of the people. As the nameless speaker points out, "nem todos participam. Muitos serão só espectadores. E outros estarão do lado de O.S., dentro de si voltarão sempre para trás" (125). As Clara later remarks, killing off O.S. will not be enough, as "um dia dirão que nunca existiu e ressuscitá-lo-ão noutro lugar com outro nome" (139). As if to underline this, the fall of Salazar/Caetano is diversified into the dethroning of a series of patriarchs, Hortense's father, the statue of "O Senhor do Mar" and Portugal's last King, Carlos I, whose assassination in 1908 heralded the start of the Republic in 1910. The conspicuous non-representation of his shooting by focusing on the moments immediately before and after it, effectively decenters it as specular foundational act and serves to recall that a public assassination was not sufficient to guarantee the future survival of the Republic's ideals.

The most sustained allegorical reproduction of the "ambivalent" revolutionary moment is the religious "Festa do Senhor do Mar. As Ana Paula Ferreira indicates, this episode "pinpoint[s] the mystifying implications that any attempt to represent the revolution as a narrative of 'popular' victory must face" (1997, 230). The revolutionary moment in Portuguese history is represented here as the interruption of the performative by the "continuist, accumulative temporality" of pedagogical time in Bhabha's schema (1990, 297) when the penitential religious procession dedicated to "O Senhor do Mar" takes an unexpected turn. As the faithful make their traditional promises, Hortense tries to imagine a balance sheet of the sacrifices "O Senhor do Mar" will exact, only to realize it is potentially limitless. The men carry the statue of "O Senhor do Mar" close to the cliff-top where it suddenly topples over for no apparent reason. Following the allegorical reading, this indicates a too passive belief that an always ambivalently structured identification will eventually, in the "nature of things", self-destruct of its own accord without conscious engagement or sustained political will.[7] As Prado Coelho remarks:

> Um dos aspectos mais curiosos de *Paisagem com mulher e mar ao fundo* é o modo como uma recusa sem ambiguidades da opressão se combina com uma consciência muito subtil da ambivalência das forças com que nos confrontamos. (21)

This ambivalence is reproduced in the stripping and unclothing of the body, the removal of the mimetic veils of ideology. The people relax and take off their uncomfortable festive costumes, becoming merely "themselves" again. The loudspeaker relays another voice and the popular celebration changes it focus but not its form. The people declare "desvendámos o enigma" exposing the order of

---

[7] As Sousa Santos remarks of the revolutionary crisis, "the state apparatus, once cleansed of its distinctly fascist features, did not collapse. It rather suffered a generalized paralysis. Because the political events had started inside it, it was 'relatively easy' to bring about the paralysis of bourgeois state power. In this sense there was no bourgeois rule. But neither, and for similar reasons, was there a proletarian rule" (1997, 42).

death as an act of phallic illusionism. The "revolta acumulada" (113) of the people brings Hortense to a new corporeal self-recognition and a restoration of voice, "mas agora eu encontro a minha voz, o meu corpo, as minhas mãos, o meu grito o meu ódio" (113-4). The wooden effigy of "O Senhor do Mar" is stripped and burned on a bonfire, hanging upside down (an historical echo with the killing of Mussolini?) in a ritualized act of sacrifice which reproduces as inversion precisely the order the people claim to displace. Indeed, his fall is readily recast in religious discourse since "é um milagre, diz o povo [...] nada do que acontece era previsível, nos termos do programa" (114). The people themselves become "os senhores do mar e os senhores da terra" (114) challenging the singularity but not the gender of the icon they have dethroned. Part Two concludes with the image of children who come running to witness "a terra dos homens em festa". This bibical echo of a false neutral assumes the literal force of its masculine inflection read in juxtaposition to the opening of Part Three, with Clara pregnant standing in front of her window as if nothing had really changed.

This silent image of Clara about to enter a spiral of depression in reverse parallel to Hortense's recovery, raises the question of Clara's political self-expression in a national cult of maternalism which the revolution will not necessarily dismantle and which has left her pregnant without social assistance or support. Neither Hortense's sexual self-discovery with Gil nor Clara's suicidal refusal of motherhood would be likely to find recognition as conventional acts of protest in the sanctioned histories of women on the left. In the final section of the novel, a dialogue recalling the dialectical structures of *Novas Cartas*, the first and second person subject status alternates between Clara and Hortense. Mirroring each other in provisional suspension of phallic law, they ask how women's resistance can be articulated through art without becoming implicated in the very mimetic structures which already enshrine their absence.[8]

---

[8] See Ana Paula Ferreira who identifies Hortense's "long-standing anti-mimetic political stance" as leading her to resist "yet another injunction to represent a political fiction [the revolution] that exists by virtue of the signifiers that decree it" (1997, 230).

Clara subjects Hortense's painting to a naive Marxist critique when she attacks her abstract, anti-mimeticism for being a bourgeois evasion of the truth, imagining instead the force of "a verdade irrompendo, balas furando as telas" (138). Yet, responding to the suggestion that she go and kill O. S. personally, Clara cannot picture herself as an assassin offering him "cogumelos venenosos," or "uma bomba mortal" (140) or waiting for him on a street corner hiding a revolver. All she can see is the comically fetishized image of a Hollywood *femme fatale* with red lipstick, high heels and a revolver, the phallic projection of O.S.'s own emasculated fear since he is commonly believed to be a eunuch (140). A woman's killing of a man, the ultimate revenge for the killing of a son or a lover in war, cannot be represented as an act of political agency where Woman, as silence and death, is structurally occluded from representation.

Gersão's own response to this impasse in *Paisagem* is to inscribe a testimonial "truth-telling" imperative into her anti-mimetic postmodern narrative through a series of breaks and reflections. In this sense, *Paisagem* effectively examines the debt which art and literature owe to the expressive acts of bearing witness to fascism. It also explores the moral boundary between rejecting fascist processes of (phallic) representation and being complicit with the destruction of representation as the last resort of human cognition at the limits of mental and physical endurance imposed by violent fascist constraint. Hortense's meditations on her abstract art in Part Two are interrupted by the disturbing thought that while she is painting, anti-Salazarist prisoners are being tortured. The intervention of a sudden "meanwhile" makes her realize, "entretanto outros ficavam de pé, dias e noites a fio, com os olhos e os braços abertos diante de uma lâmpada acesa, cambaleando, ébrios de cansaço" (74). This moment of negative epiphany mirrors *en abyme* the project of *Paisagem* itself as a postmodern testimony to the many different forms which Salazarist torture took. Hortense is effectively forced to delimit her aesthetics in necessary relation to the political imperative of bearing witness to violence. In defining the referential limits of the literary in terms of its relationship to Latin American testimonial discourse, Alberto Moreiras has usefully written that:

> The specificity of testimonio, and its particular position in the
> current cultural configuration, depend upon an extraliterary
> stance or moment, which we could also understand as a
> moment of arrest of all symbolization in a direct appeal to the
> non-exemplary, but still singular, pain beyond any possibility
> of representation. Testimonio is testimonio because it suspends
> the literary at the very same time that is constitutes itself as a
> literary act: as literature, it is a liminal event opening onto a
> nonrepresentational, drastically indexed order of experience.
> (195)

Refusing the emplotment of teleological history and the fixing of specular images, Hortense makes writing a renaming, healing force and a didactic return to first principles as the new born child in *Paisagem* experiences "o choque da sombra contra a luz" (147). As a testimony to collective suffering which nonetheless foregrounds Hortense's and Clara's experiences as women, *Paisagem* moves to remember literature itself as a liminal event demarcating the edge of Moreiras's "drastically indexed order of experience" (195). Working along the border between testimonial memory and the *Künstlerroman* topos of "artist/writer coming to voice" *Paisagem* uses its artistic epiphany in the feminine to simulate a collective return to expression, which is simultaneously constrained by post-revolutionary anxiety regarding the political and psychoanalytical limits of representation. In the next chapter, Hélia Correia's *Montedemo* shows the end of maritime empire detailed in *Paisagem* giving way to a new fascination with the land and with Portugal's archaeological and ethnographic roots (Pintasilgo 1986, 69). At the same time, however this serves Correia as a pretext to continue exploring the issue of feminine alterity on a more universalized level within, and as a condition of, collective and individual expression in the socio-symbolic contract of community.

CHAPTER 3

Hélia Correia's *Montedemo*: The Tale of an (Un)becoming Virgin

When they sang your lament in triplicate
In words familiar and intimate

The litany of limb and feature by destroyed mothers
Stopped the hand of Gods and artists. (O'Malley 2)

Hélia Correia's *Montedemo* portrays the type of unchanging rural peasant community to which many of the scattered colonial diaspora described in *Paisagem* eventually "returned". Reflecting Correia's interests in narrative fiction and theatre this novella was published in 1983 and subsequently successfully dramatized by João Brites for "O Bando" in 1987 as an outdoor production staged in Tondela and Lisbon.[1] As the publicity material for the production in Tondela points out to its intended audience, "em Portugal existe uma forte tradição popular marcada pelo conto. Transportar o espírito inventivo e

---

[1] Partly in response to Correia's focus on matriarchy and the culturally repressed feminine body, Teresa Horta reviewed Correia's work in the 1980s as exemplary of "escrita feminina". See Horta 1983. Sceptical about aesthetic separatism, Hélia Correia rather emphasizes the influence of class-consciousness and Communist resistance to fascism:

> Não considero determinante que, pelo facto de ser uma mulher a escrever, a sua escrita possua uma qualquer tipicidade a que se chame feminina [....]. Além disso, a mulher é um ser humano e social e as marcas que recebe não são exclusivamente femininas. Fui muito mais marcada, na infância e adolescência, pela minha condição de classe. (Louro 1983, 27)

See also Letria and França for Correia's comments on feminism and women's writing.

imaginativo do conto para o campo teatral não é mais do que: 'pôr as coisas no seu devido lugar'". Drawing on the symbiosis of Christian and pre-Christian elements in Portuguese popular religions *Montedemo* traces the emergence of a new collective narrative in response to inexplicable supernatural phenomena in a small Portuguese seaside town in the post-revolutionary period.[2] Exploring Christianity's syncretic negotiation with, and only partial superseding of, ancient cults which celebrated fertility rites, Correia demonstrates what happens when this always precarious cultural equilibrium overbalances and chaos is temporarily unleashed.[3]

The story is set in a village somewhere on Portugal's Atlantic coast, and also near a mountain popularly known by the local people as Montedemo. Like Lídia Jorge's well-known novel of the rural Algarve, *O Dia dos Prodígios*, *Montedemo* describes the kind of world the revolution has barely touched. However, although the village resists the external forces of change, it proves none the less liable to be destabilized from within by seismic shifts in its own founding symbolisms. A repressed elderly spinster, Dona Ercília Silveira, believes that she is keeping a tight rein on her plain, unmarried, middle-aged niece Milena, who goes to the annual carnival, the Festa de São Jorge, and returns transfigured. Her aunt prepares to throw her out on discovering that she is pregnant, only for the increasingly luminous Milena to pre-empt this authoritarian move by going to live in a hut on the sands, on the edge of the village, adopting

---

[2] In interview with Eduardo J. Brum and José F. Tavares, Correia identifies the specific setting of the work as the originally pagan, "dia de São Brás" festival which occurs annually in February near Nazaré. Celebrating the end of winter and the coming of spring, it marks the beginning of the carnival season with mascarades and communal festivities, as well as pilgrimages and petitions to São Brás.

[3] See Kristeva 1986b, 177-8 on Freud and the Archaic Mother, and 181-2 on reconciling matrilinearism with systems of exchange. See Warner 276-284, especially 277, on the Virgin assuming the functions of Hera and Demeter. See Pazos Alonso 1999a for an enlightening reading of *Montedemo* in relation to the works of Portuguese anthropologist, Moisés Espírito Santo.

as her friend the village madwoman Irene.[4] She refuses all medical assistance or religious correction and is befriended by Dulcinha and Tenório, a spinster and bachelor in late middle-age who fall in love and marry, under the inspiring influence of her transgression. Milena's marginal existence is tolerated by the village until she gives birth to a mysterious black child and insists on feeding him in public view. The wrath of the village descends on Milena in the form of a mob, her hut goes up in flames and she mysteriously disappears with her child in the midst of natural upheavals which shake the heavens. Passing into local mythology, her shrine is visited by Dulcinha and Tenório, she appears as visions and her story becomes a parable of boundless love always threatening to exceed and disrupt the authority of the church fathers. Milena digresses from the traditional fertility rites common to popular religious manifestations by exceeding the permitted boundaries of containment within carnivalesque ritual and engendering a new cycle of oral symbolization.

Montedemo uses Milena's story to describe the negotiation, breakdown and reaffirmation of the socio-symbolic contract which holds together a village otherwise characterized by the disruptive forces of "naufrágios, emigrações e loucos sem abrigo" (12). The community defines its coherence in opposition to a violent history of death, departure, hysteria and nomadic non-settlement. Given that the discipline and control of the maternal body are central to the ascendancy of paternal Christian agency in establishing a phallically ordered society such as the village in Montedemo, the novella centres on the return of the repressed mother through fertility rites celebrating maternity. The principle critical focus for my analysis is therefore derived from the psychoanalytical theories of Julia Kristeva, particularly the history and semiotics of virgin worship in "Stabat Mater" and the theories of abjection advanced in Powers of Horror.[5] In her

---

[4] See Sadlier for interesting readings of Montedemo and its immediate predecessor, O Número dos Vivos, in terms of Gothic literary influences and Freudian sexual repression. See also Urbano Tavares Rodrigues for discussion of madness and flight paradigms in Correia's fiction.

[5] In a 1987 interview for Diário de Notícias Correia told Elisabete França, "acompanhei muito a onda das feministas francesas e americanas" (V). In discussion with the present author in

"Stabat Mater", Kristeva reads Christianity's traditional reduction of femininity to maternity as a particularly powerful and refined manifestation of fantasized regression to primary narcissism, the desire for return to union with the pre-signifying maternal semiotic. Kristeva's concept of the "semiotic" as opposed to "the imaginary" in Lacanian theory, refers to the rhythmic, sonic dimension of language associated with, and driven by, the shifting energy forces of a womb-like space which Kristeva, adapting from Plato, terms the "chora" (Moi 12-13). This "semiotic", closely linked with the physical, bodily origins of language, is therefore prior to and always positioned outside the symbolic order of meaning as mediated by the paternal law which guarantees subjectivity.[6] Consequently, it is not able to signify within the phallic order, but can only pressurize, traverse or disrupt it from a position of otherness.

Applying this to poetic and/as theoretical practice, "Stabat Mater" reviews Christian maternalism in terms of the cultural and artistic interdependence between the symbolic and the semiotic, evident in the uses religion makes of music, art and ritual as sources of emotional appeal. Kristeva's typographical division of "Stabat Mater" creates two parallel columns, such that the scholarly mastery of the symbolic on the right runs alongside a fluid poetics of maternal experience on the left, the artistic flow of the semiotic. However, the risk in Kristeva's terms is that the semiotic will run out of control and the resulting collapse of the phallic order will lead to an unhealthy resurgence of anarchy and chaos. Thus, although maternal "jouissance" is particularly closely aligned with the impulses of creativity, music and art it must, for Kristeva, remain disciplined by phallic symbolization (1986b, 163; 1986c, 204-5). Controversially, therefore, from the perspective of feminist agency, Kristeva locates the feminine outside the

---

2000, Correia indicated that Kristeva's works did figure among her readings in the 1970s and 1980s and that she had been particularly impressed by *Powers of Horror*.

[6] See Justo who reads *Montedemo* as undermining Christian phallogocentrism by demonstrating that "o conhecimento não vem do céu, não é azul nem possui o esplendor da aurora boreal, é um longo e penoso recolhimento sobre o que é, sobre os momentos imediatamente anteriores ao ser, funde-se com o prazer e o desejo, é o seu próprio espelho" (12).

symbolic order, speaking only in relation to the symbolic as its transgressive, disruptive outside. As she puts it:

> If the feminine *exists*, it only exists in the order of significance or signifying process, and it is only in relation to meaning and signification, positioned as their excessive or transgressive other that it *exists, speaks, thinks* (itself) and *writes* (itself) for both sexes. (Moi 11)

Correia's text describes and enacts Kristeva's dilemma of language for the expression of the maternal feminine in the western religious symbolic. In *Montedemo*, as in Kristeva's theories, the signifying conventions of representational discourse retain the upper hand but not without acknowledging a debt owed to, and a certain constitutive pressure from, an unsymbolizable otherness which makes it absence felt. The semi-ironic perspective of a third person extraheterodiegetic narrator maintains a fine balance throughout the novella between satire and complicity in relaying the unconscious lapses and illogicalities of the villagers' reactions to events. *Montedemo* opens epigraphically with Hamlet's famous anti-rational declaration to Horatio: "Há mais coisas no céu e na terra, Horácio, do que a tua filosofia pode conceber". *Montedemo* similarly points beyond its own epistemological boundaries to mysteries left unexplained, as the rational utterances of representational narrative are punctuated with statements of silence and ellipsis gesturing towards the inexpressible in Judeo-Christian tradition and Greco-Roman myth effectively echoed by the novella's densely intertextual poetics. The result, as I will argue, is a weaving in and out of the religious symbolic which leaves the fragility of its boundaries and the sacrificial cost of its installation throughout history more clearly delineated, if not actually displaced.

Montedemo opens by positing with the words "tudo começou"(15), a mysterious "something" that has implicitly already happened but is only retrievable through memory. As if to question the very concept of the teleological origins of narrative, the text starts precisely with a lack of consensus as to "when it all began", since only "alguns lembraram" (15) that it all started on a dry Sunday when the earth trembled. The tremor is a gentle subterranean disruption of the earth's surface linked to the subconscious world of dream and imagination, manifesting itself just before dawn, the time of "moribundos e bêbedos, todos pensando que se balouçavam em líquidos maternos, quentes e protectores" (15). This reference to the uterine pre-symbolic, the semiotic space, indicates that the ambiguous signal of the earth tremor and the ensuing events will defy the order of rational explanation. The tremor is followed by further portents and supernatural signs, such as the sudden disappearance of all the cats, which others see as the beginning of it all. The tension between unruly nature and the overlapping epistemologies of science and religion becomes evident in the terms used to account for the prodigies.

The exodus of the cats gives way to the breaking of great purple waves on the beach resembling the robe worn by Christ in the passion procession, as if nature were reclaiming the sacred symbolisms of religious cult. The rational-minded representatives of the community, Tenório the pharmacist and Esteves the scribe, offer scientific explanations such as those which accounted for the Nile's flowing red in the plagues of Egypt. Yet even the more educated are not immune to primal childlike fear when faced with the limits of their ability to control the physical universe through religion or science. The repetition of "contam" and "dizem alguns" is the necessary, comforting voice of oral tradition, the Kristevan "sujet-en-procès" of a community in a childlike state. Echoing the Book of Genesis and the plagues of Egypt the chapter concludes "ao quarto dia madrugou o mar com seus tons de cinzento e espumas altas" (17) and life seems to return to normal, but for the astral predictions of even greater wonders from the village madwoman Irene.

The celebration of the "Festa de São Jorge", the annual carnival, constitutes an uneasy truce between the Christian fathers and the earlier associations of the place derived from the special properties of Montedemo as a magical source of fertility and pre-marital blessing. The mountain's vegetation follows a cycle of seething growth and decay described here in terms of masculine sexuality, "inchar e encolher, como ofegante, como homem desvairado de desejo" (19). The name the people give the mountain is a sexually suggestive conjoining of devil and mounting, describing "um garrano aceso e índio que não estava na terra para que o montassem santos, ainda que cavaleiros" (20-21). Playing on the word "montar" or "mount", Montedemo is likened to a spirited Arab horse which no saint, not even a knight or cavalier saint, can mount or tame. The church renames the mountain Saõ Jorge in order to bring its practices under the control of a dragon-slayer saint, himself semi-mythical and born of ambiguous pre-Christian origins. However, as if a curse rested upon the site, no attempt to build a chapel there ever succeeds. The people, the church and the mountain are left in a state of unstable equilibrium, "meia guerra ganha e outra meia perdida" (21).

The "Festa de São Jorge" comes around on the second Sunday in February, also the period of the Mardi Gras carnival, emphasizing the progression of the story through the cycle of the months and seasons. The villagers' true selves emerge from behind costumes and masking. The young are drawn into a bacchanalian frenzy of wine, dance, music and frenetic coupling. The permitted token return of the body, the making of love and children beyond the sanction of church law, is frowned on but tolerated by the older generation. Indeed, the tapping of their feet to the music marks their unconscious, physical acquiesence with the rhythmic pulsions of ongoing life. The "festa" thus demarcates the boundary of communal signification and the corresponding limits of oral memory as the narrator remarks, "o que há para além disso, e há tanta coisa, nunca foi perguntado ou respondido. Porque aquilo que as palavras não cobriram, mesmo que exista, não se reproduz" (22).

The carnival installs the unstable boundary which characterizes the process of abjection, central to the theories of cultural taboo which Kristeva articulates in *Powers of Horror*. Abjection, as Kristeva defines it, is the usually ritualized process by which matter considered to be culturally impure or filthy must be expelled from the body in order for signification and social identity to be established. The fact that "the abject" never can be totally expelled places it on the borders of meaning, identity and community as an omnipresent, threatening force and a zone of ambiguity. In the Judaic traditions which Kristeva observes, abjection is specifically associated with the maternal body, "that 'improper and unclean' place, which is the maternal living being" (1982,104) and which must be disavowed as a precondition of speech. In Christianity, abjection is specifically bound up with the conceptualization of sin in what Kristeva terms a "dialectic elaboration, as it becomes integrated in the Christian Word as a threatening otherness – but always nameable, always totalizeable" (17). This otherness goes beyond the nameable and the totalizable in *Montedemo,* as the "Festa de São Jorge" temporarily suspends the customary boundaries of sin and the carnival is played out figuratively as maternal, semiotic space.

As the music and wine-drinking gather momentum, the people feel momentarily liberated from their subjection to original sin, the fundamental Judeo-Christian split of good and evil, as they descend into a bacchanalian delirium that no-one can explain or name. This chapter opens with a radical break, a phrase for which there is no immediate syntactical referent as "juram alguns que foi às três da tarde, às três exactas horas da tarde de S. Jorge" (23). The intertextual echo is of Christ dying on the cross to redeem mankind from original sin, but here the people are suddenly "nascidos sem pecado" (23) in a return to primal unity with maternal, pre-symbolic space, "como se fosse a vida leite e espuma" (23). The music to which the villagers dance sounds as if it were bubbling through the water and mingling with the waves of the sea, enhancing the rhythmic properties of both.

> Pareceu que de repente a música da banda soava dentro de água, aos borbotões, entre os ais do golfinho e os risos da medusa, e ali estava o abismo: - Que é isto, Virgem Santa? - Nervura de corais, fulgores de rocha. O verde e o negro, o nácar salvador.(23)

The dance restores the people to a state of pre-lapsarian bliss as they lose their sense of physical gravity and think "estamos nos balançando, livres de todo o peso, diria até" (23). This is foreshadowed by the weightlessness of the sea in the first chapter where "o próprio mar parecia tão sem peso, tão dançarino e limpo de pecado" (15). The "Virgem Santa" is juxtaposed with the lethal, castrating fear of the snake-haired Medusa of classical myth.[7] The "nácar" of the mother of pearl which foresees Milena's resplendent pregnancy, acquires new properties of salvation. The euphoria is broken, however, with the phrase "que delírio foi esse? Ninguém sabe" (23). Overcome by an inchoate terror of darkness and shame, the people flee the mountain in silence collectively repressing the events of the day.

While the first part of the novella focuses on the collective identity and belief-systems of the village, the emphasis shifts following the "Festa de São Jorge" to a group of individuals who find themselves variously transfigured. Milena, the magic catalyst of these changes, had seemed to be a confirmed virginal spinster, "a rapariga decente: nem modas, nem namoros, nem pinturas na cara. Talvez um tudo-nada decente em demasia" (25). It is her puritanical aunt, D. Ercília Silveira, who unwittingly suggests that Milena's extreme "decency" will tip over into passionate excess. Milena has ironically been sent to the "festa" at Montedemo as a possible antidote to her emaciation, which D. Ercília blames on her unfulfilled mystical fervour, "a falta de um convento", as she thinks with a suggestive ellipsis "e é por isso que está a definhar..." (26). She becomes unwittingly complicit with Milena's undoing through her friendship with the Ferrão sisters, who have expertise in herbal medicines and whose suggestion it is that Milena go to the "Festa de São Jorge". Whilst D. Ercília worries about her niece's late homecoming she recollects her own prohibited lovemaking with "o Tó cauteleiro", reiterating the mountain's association with pre-lapsarian freedom, "ele e ela, das épocas lendárias em que eram um só ser" (26). The overlap between the two women's lives reveals the deepest repression masking the wildest of passions in D. Ercília's past, all the more satirically underlined because the very vocation of the lottery ticket salesman is to endorse the victory of chaos and chance over order and predictability.

Milena returns home from the "festa" with "o vestido rasgado na cintura" (27). The emphasis on the area of Milena's waist echoes the symbolic significance of the Virgin Mary's sash in Catholic iconography. As Marina

---

[7] See Pazos Alonso 1999a for a reading which draws on the theories of Hélène Cixous.

Warner writes in her tracing of pagan antecedents for the sash as enhancing fertility, "the sexuality of the symbol derives from its tantalizing ambivalence: loosed, the girdle gives promise; fastened, it denies" (279). Milena's pregnancy brings about her striking transformation into an icon of life and beauty, attracting the desire of men, the envy of women and the friendship of the lunatic, Irene. When Milena leaves D. Ercília's house and goes to live in Irene's hut at the edge of the village, the twin facets of the maternal feminine, the worshipped and the abjected, are placed in harmonious cohabitation, preparing for their structural role switch at the end of the novella.

Milena is described as a vision of whiteness, light and beauty and wears a constant enigmatic smile (32, 40). Her "beleza indecifrável"(37) and her "rosto alucinante, doloroso de olhar-se como o rosto de Deus" (40) evoke the ineffable in the Christian tradition, recalling Kristeva's description of the sublime as a means of keeping the abject under control (1982, 11). Behind the image of the virgin, however, are the powers of Aphrodite, the Greek love goddess who inspires others to uncontrollable passion. Irene, in contrast, is a chrone-like figure, characterized by ugliness and anarchic laughter. She is feared as a source of disorder and chaos, committing the besetting sin of Eve as "altas horas andava por pomares roubando fruta e emudecendo os cães com meios que ninguém conseguia perceber" (35). Along this boundary of separation as signification, the two women themselves do not articulate symbolic language, forming a non-verbal community in apposition to the inadequate explanations of events given by the men of knowledge. Irene speaks through animal noises and laughter, reading astral signs and currents "por baixo do silêncio" (45). Milena is predominantly silent, expressing her feelings through her smile and facial expressions. Their hut, which smells of straw and animals, evokes the traditional Christian image of the crib. However, gifts are brought not by a wise man, but by the wise woman Dulcinha who knows about herbal medicines. The crib becomes an alternative matrifocal space, inspiring the conversion of Tenório, the bachelor pharmacist, to new forms of wisdom.

Dulcinha subverts village convention by falling in love and opting to marry Tenório, in spite of their relatively advanced years. As the anticlerical freethinker, Tenório represents the traditional historical focus of opposition to religious tyranny. Supplanted by Milena, however, he can no longer pose as a modern, secular god serving the women in his shop who used to approach him "com as mãos postas em adoração" (39). Just as Tenório is saved from the hyper-rationalism of science, Dulcinha escapes the strictures of orthodox religious dogma. Whilst Milena's transgression arises from reproducing outside wedlock, Dulcinha's decision to marry conversely flouts the sexual economy because it had written her off as no longer reproductive. Asserting the value of heterosexual love for its own non-reproductive sake, she expresses desire in the comically displaced form of uncontrollable spending "em caprichos histéricos de noiva" (48). This leads her to quarrel with her sister, Isaura, the use of whose car she will lose by marriage as Isaura asserts "eu não trocava um carro velho nem por um homem de trinta anos" (47). Isaura recovers all that Dulcinha takes from their joint account by doing her washing at Dulcinha's home every Sunday for years to come and keeping accounts. This return of a strictly symmetrical economy of exchange foreshadows the rebalancing of cultural forces that will ultimately restore order following Milena's act of transgression.

The climax of the villagers' fear provides the turning point of the novella. Their uncertainty proliferates as mysterious fires break out like will-o' the wisps spreading over people's rooftops and vanishing before the firemen arrive on the scene. The fires melt plastic objects and to the people's horror, even religious artefacts such as "figurinhas de santas, crucifixos, as senhoras de Fátima" (44) are not immune. As the villagers spy on Dulcinha, Tenório and Milena, the idea of a collective ritual sacrifice is insinuated into their minds as the only way to restore social cohesion. The village retreats into itself becoming increasingly hermetic to outsiders and visitors, keeping their "eventos demoníacos" to themselves, "longe de intromissões de forasteiros" (50). Where the social contract is, in Kristeva's analysis, founded on sacrificial relations of separation and the articulation of differences (1986c, 199), the feared regenerative body of women acts as the scapegoat or abject which the social organism requires in order to signify itself as communicable meaning.

The ostensible catalyst for this act of community is provided when Milena's child is inexplicably born black and she feeds him in public. Esteves, the scribe, tries to pacify the newly-awakened fears of the village by satirizing the old superstition that Milena could have produced a mulatto child, "só por obra do diabo" (49) and providing the rational solution that she was seduced "por algum retornado das antigas colónias" (50). The villagers have never seen Milena interested in any man and therefore cannot imagine her with "aqueles negros bêbedos e pobres, carregados de filhos e incapazes de levar na conversa fosse que mulher fosse" (50). The Catholic beatification of the maternal, imaged throughout the novella in terms of radiant whiteness, is exposed here not only as the obverse of the violently rejected maternal body, but also as the color-blind myth of a white racist society. The narrator remarks:

> Aquela exibição de um corpo feminino com sua nudez implácavel; essa criança escura, parida sem ter nome, raça ou paternidade, foram um desafio que a vila, enfurecida, não pode ignorar. Tinham os habitantes atingido aquele estado em que a insegurança inventa, do seu nada, recursos bestiais de força e crueldade. (51)

The exposure of the female breast, feeding the child in public, triggers the final destructive outrage of the crowd, faced with the infantile insecurity of their own physical fragility. Kristeva points to milk and tears in the cult of the madonna as "the metaphors of non-speech, of a 'semiotics' that linguistic communication does not account for. The Mother and her attributes, evoking sorrowful humanity, thus become representatives of a 'return of the repressed' in monotheism" (1986b, 174). The maternal and colonial bodies, historically repressed under Salazarism, return only to be all the more violently re-repressed in the affirmation of more fundamental cultural taboo. The community moves as a monolithic "one", a single monstrous body, to exorcize its fear of chaos as diversity, the splitting and multiplying of the regenerative female body as a "brimming of the flesh" (Kristeva 1982, 126) beyond white male control (1982,

77-8). The monolithic power of the phallus is here evoked through the collective grouping of the people into the formation of a snake, like "orgãos, tecidos, de um enorme animal, uma serpente. Uma serpente, um réptil gigantesco" (52). At the same time, however, the defining limits of the community are shown to be arbitrary and fragile when the phalanx scatters and each terrified individual pursues Milena according to their own hatreds and fears. The "reason" for Milena's disappearance among the angry crowd remains a mystery as the earth itself intervenes and quakes three times, evoking the death of Christ, green lightning flashes from Montedemo, and the sea runs red in a series of tidal waves. The black child disappears with Milena as the hut burns down and leaves no trace of its inhabitants, and the tremors of the earth close the cycle of prodigies which they began. The manner of Milena's "death" is figuratively akin to the assumption of the Virgin Mary who is spared bodily decay and returns to the faithful through apparitions and visions.

Irene returns to the village physically rejuvenated some months after Milena's disappearance, "muito calma e dotada de um sorriso que lhe desenrugava a pele do rosto" (55). She superficially emulates the laws of Christianity, directing her prayers and genuflections at the sun, and moving in and out of the community like the "aves migratórias" (56). The space where her cabin once stood becomes "um espaço de brilho negro" (56) in which flowers continue to bloom from the ashes. In the alchemical transformation wrought by Milena's fate, Irene is accepted by the community who "receavam-na tanto que optaram por amá-la" (55). The boundary is redrawn and its relative positionings are reassigned in the aftermath of violent abjection, as "'subject' and 'object' [community and counter-community] push each other away, confront each other, collapse, and start again" (Kristeva 1982, 18). Tenório and Dulcinha do not mourn Milena's disappearance but are seen taking her offerings at night The "Festa de São Jorge" never takes place again. There are reported sightings of Milena and her child as "há quem tenha avistado uma mulher belísima levando ao colo um rapazinho escuro por entre o fervilhar do matagal" (56). Tenório refuses the closure of meaning or interpretation stating "não há limites para o que é humano" (56).

Structured cyclically as a new oral "myth", *Montedemo* destabilizes its already semi-satirical position of authority by referring to the repressed, semiotic gaps and exclusions of its own coming to voice. The catalytic "events" which precipitate the story of *Montedemo* are never actually spoken or represented as such. The climax which occurs with Milena's persecution is prefaced with "contam", rhythmically repeated three times, and used to exemplify the transformative effects of retelling, as "tantas vezes passou pelas palavras, pelos sonhos, pelo secreto transtorno da vaidade que vai tomando formas improváveis, como as grandes cores móveis do delírio" (51). The novella itself thus emerges as a synthesis of different oral versions, the symbolic organizing of multiple narrative drives into a synthetic, written whole which is conscious of its fragile status. The strong traces of orality in the narrator's mode of address emphasize the aural and the listener rather than the reader, recalling the Catholic significance afforded the mother as listener, as the recipient, maternal ear of Kristeva's virgin, who intercedes with God on behalf of humanity (1986b). The oral and aural are intimately connected to the somatic, pre-symbolic sounds of maternal space.

In her essay on "Women's Time" Kristeva warns of the dangers inherent in feminists' founding an idealized counter-society on the concept of "an archaic, full, total englobing mother with no frustration, no separation, with no break-producing symbolism (with no castration in other words)" (1986c, 205). The "épocas lendárias" of just such an archaic Mother Goddess appear, on one level, to inform the repeating temporal cycles which resist the effects of separation and castration in the figurative patterns of Milena's story. Following her expulsion from D. Ercília's house, Milena is likened to a skittish goat which appears on the sands, "de *ágeis pernas doiradas,* orgulhosas, como colunas sustentando o mundo" (35-6, my italics). D. Ercília's correspondingly describes her younger self as "uma bem amada rapariga, cabelos de *oiro,* saias de organdi sopradas pelo vento contra as *pernas* gulosas, *leves e finas pernas de gazela*" (26, my italics). The year itself is cyclical and seasonally bound in this tourist town which lives from the activities of fishing and the perennial return of the sunshine. The erasure of linear time is compounded by vagueness about age. Only D. Ercília is unequivocally sixty years old and, in keeping with her outward Catholic devotion, she adheres to the orthodoxy of Anno Domini and its chronology. Irene, however, possesses a "feio rosto sem idade" (36) and it is stated of Tenório that "a idade - que mal se lhe notava porque nunca soubera parecer jovem - tornara-o saturado de ciências" (40). Dulcinha Ferrão is the younger of the two sisters but physically considerably the larger and therefore mocked by the diminutive ending of her name, "que lhe ficava tão desalinhado como um laço de seda na cabeça" (41). Milena is vaguely "trinta e tais" or even "trinta e muitos" (30) in the eyes of the fishermen, but the name Milena invokes the word "milénio" as she is pursued by angry villagers "corcovados os ombros nas tarefas tão milenárias da destruição" (52).

Montedemo's maternal subversion of chronological, historical time recalls Kristeva's separation of linear historical time from women's time, that of repetition and eternity, as tangential to history (1986c, 189-91) and the hierarchical arrangement of conventional realist narrative, whereby historical time takes precedence, is interestingly reversed. The timeless cycle of maternal reproduction dominates only to be occasionally and surprisingly interrupted,as if "anachronistically", by identifiable historical references such as the Republic, increased liberalism, the *retornados* from the colonial war, and the growing impact of tourism. The narrative drive of the work is not towards teleological closure or endings, but towards a constantly reiterated present, "ainda hoje" and the ending is the open-ended imperative of boundless love. Dulcinha quotes Milena in conclusion, "amem-se", diz Dulcinha, "nunca se sabe o fim" (56). The inspiration of Milena, the continued pressure of the maternal body against the separation that installs signification, thus remains despite the regulatory "cães e gases" (56) which Tenório fears will suppress her memory, but on what conditions does she return? Placing the Maternal in tangential apposition to history, *Montedemo* effectively poses Kristeva's feminist dilemma between acceptance of "*insertion* into history and the radical *refusal* of the subjective limitations imposed by this history's time on an experiment carried out in the name of the irreducible difference" (1986c, 195).

Satirizing the reactionary nature of the rural "povo" in whose capacity for transformation Marxist intellectuals had believed, *Montedemo* shows how the maternal body continues, in the post-revolutionary world, to demarcate an ambivalent zone on the border of abjection and desire, a barely assimilable difference which returns only as myth. The oppressed black *retornado*, in contrast, acts as a warning from history, affording a timely reminder of the Colonial War as well as a link between abjection and racial otherness which goes beyond Kristeva's general frame of reference. In this respect, Dulcinha, Tenório and Irene clearly function didactically at the end of the novella as the only figures to have shown a capacity for transformation beyond primal fears and irrational hatreds such as those associated with racism.

The dramatic productions of *Montedemo* staged at night in Lisbon and Tondela significantly emphasized the interchangeability of roles and identities, as the masking and cloaking of the cast and the outdoor walkabout format sought to interpellate the audience into a new "community in the making". As Tito Lívio described it, "a subversão instala-se na aldeia e estende-se ao cenário, fragmentado, descontínuo, fascinante no seu percurso, pois cada um pode escolher melhor o seu ângulo de visão dos acontecimentos (33). The directly oral appeal of *Montedemo,* as literature and as theatre, effectively raises in an extreme parabolic format the question of the terms on which women could be reinscribed into the narrative time of history, by plumbing the repressive depths of the socio-symbolic investments at stake in renegotiating such transactions. The texts by Olga Gonçalves and Lídia Jorge discussed in the next two chapters move to affirm the woman writer as creative individual in relation to, but no longer necessarily as a function of, the renegotiation of society and signification which the revolutionary crisis had seemed to permit. These two writers adopt different perspectives on the possibilities offered by the women's *Künstlerroman* format as a "coming to re/presentation" engaged in the literary renarrativization of history.

CHAPTER 4

Testaments of Youth: Olga Gonçalves's *Mandei-lhe uma Boca* and *Sara*

> Bem sei que a revolta da mulher é a que leva a convulsão em todos os extractos sociais; nada fica de pé, nem relações de classe, nem de grupo, nem individuais.... E o problema da mulher, no meio disto, não é o de perder ou ganhar, é o da sua identidade. (Barreno et al. 231)

Olga Gonçalves's two novels, *Mandei-lhe uma Boca* and *Sara,* published nine years apart in 1977 and 1986 respectively, may be read as twin volumes in a two part female *Bildungsroman.* Adding a specifically gendered dimension to Gonçalves's established literary stance as "a cronista da Revolução" (1987, 24) they chart the impact of post-25 April social transformations on Portuguese youth from a feminine-focalized perspective.[1] In *Mandei-lhe uma Boca,* the heroine and narrator, Sara, is sixteen years old and in open revolt against her parents as she

---

[1] See Bulger for a short but insightful reading of *Sara* as marking social change in gender roles. See Gonçalves's interview with Graciete Besse in which she speaks strongly in support of women's struggle for emancipation. See Silva-Brummel's reading of *Mandei-lhe uma Boca* and *Sara* which analyzes Sara as "die neue portugiesische Frau" (134) ("the new Portuguese woman"). See also Gonçalves's article for *Mulheres* in 1987 where she asks herself parenthetically:

> (serei eu, talvez, uma das muitas mulheres que, não sentindo a necessidade de se afirmar feminista, leva a mulher para as suas páginas, querendo perpetuar-lhe os reflexos de uma coragem que todos reconhecemos como soberana?) (25).

begins to see through the sexual hypocrisies and infidelities of the middle-aged, middle-class professional couples of Lisbon society. This short novel is effectively a prolonged oral monologue which constitutes Sara's side of a conversation with her mother's old school friend Riva, conducted over the course of a weekend spent in Riva's Lisbon flat. *Sara* continues the story of *Mandei-lhe uma Boca* eight years later when Sara is in her twenties and completing her university studies in philosophy.

Both *Mandei-lhe uma Boca* and *Sara* represent the generation of the post-revolutionary decade, increasingly cut adrift from the ideals and inspirations of the 1970s. Parents and children are experimenting with new forms of relationship as the paternalistic, authoritarian hierarchies of the Estado Novo seem outmoded. As Laura Bulger points out, in *Sara* "destaca-se a representação da figura feminina sujeita, por um lado, às convenções dum patriarquismo tradicional [...] e, por outro, às incertezas que se geram numa sociedade em transformação" (11). In this transitional dialectic of tradition and modernity, women are caught between a sense of liberation and betrayal. They enjoy the double-edged gifts of the sexual revolution and the end of Catholic family hegemony as micro-unit of state authority, but they have been left uncertain as to what type of family relations will replace it. The sociologist Boaventura de Sousa Santos has written of the late 1970s period of transition that it ran "at different paces according to the different areas of social practice. Such a period of transition manifests itself in significant inconsistencies, disjunctures, or discrepancies" (34). In contrast to *Novas Cartas*, the break in generational continuity and the lack of genealogical roots are represented as problematic in *Mandei-lhe uma Boca* and *Sara,* positing the threat to family-based identity as a potential loss of stable, social organization. What Maria de Lourdes Pintasilgo described as the post-revolutionary "desvio em relação à norma" produced widespread social panic at the same time as it expanded the potential margins of innovation (1986, 64). Where a sense of social alienation and anomy come to the fore, it is perhaps not surprising that these two novels mark a return to identity formation fictions such as those typified by the *Bildungsroman* genre. Gonçalves, significantly in this context, admits to a strong, formative influence from Simone de Beauvoir, the French feminist writer whose work she translated into Portuguese.[2]

The appropriation and redefinition by women writers of the generic norms established by male-authored *Bildungsroman* have provided a major focus of interest for Anglo-American feminist criticism in the last two decades.[3] Many of the common narrative themes and preoccupations identified by this area of study are evident in Gonçalves's treatment of the genre. Indeed, Gonçalves interestingly incorporates a metafictional English influence in Sara's literary genealogy through her mentor Riva who is also a writer and, like Gonçalves herself, spent a number of years living in England. In both texts, Sara's relationship with Riva provides the focus for her discussion of literary and personal disorientation and the lack of viable role models, a position effectively mirrored and compounded, as will become evident, by Riva's own somewhat exceptional position in relation to conventional society. The conflict between women's personal development and their integration into society is a recurrent problem for woman-centred *Bildungsromane* where male-authored prototypes such as Goethe's *Wilhelm Meister's Apprenticeship* (Abel et al. 4-6; Labovitz 3) emphasize social integration as the proper culmination of the spiritual development of inner potential. As critics of the genre have pointed out, the very concept of women using their freedom to learn, develop and engage meaningfully with society as "world beyond family" is often precisely what is at stake in

___

[2] In interview with Eduarda Chiote for *Letras e Letras* in 1988, Gonçalves commented, "foi depois de traduzir *La Femme Rompue* e *L'Âge de Discrétion*, no mesmo volume, que me dei conta da monumental lição que recebera da escritora [Simone de Beauvoir] " (12).

[3] My definitions of feminine *Bildungsroman* are derived from three main sources. I draw on the discussions of female development fiction edited by Elizabeth Abel, Marianne Hirsch and Elizabeth Langland, on Annis Pratt's analysis of the women's development novel in terms of archetypal patterns, and on Esther Kleinbord Labovitz's close readings of four twentieth-century women writers of *Bildungsromane,* including Simone de Beauvoir. Significantly, none of these refers to the Spanish picaresque as part of the male-voiced, male-authored tradition which they are seeking to redefine. Gonçalves's Sara explicitly distances herself from an Iberian *Bildungsroman* prototype in *Lazarillo de Tormes* and is more inspired, as we will see, by the anglophone American model of Alice Walker's *The Color Purple*.

female-authored *Bildungroman* (Labovitz 2-3, 137, 246-7; Abel et al. 6-7, 10-11). This dilemma for women is manifested most clearly in the tension between marital and/or sexual fulfilment, and intellectual and/or professional opportunity which introduces split, ambivalent structures, a tendency for the heroine to retreat to an inner world, and an avoidance of narrative closure (Labovitz 6). As Abel et al. remark, "even the broadest definitions of the *Bildungsroman* presuppose a range of social options available only to men" (7). A common strategy which female protagonists use to resolve the conflict between the intellectual/spiritual development of the "inner" world, and the adoption of a social role required by the "outer" one, is to become artists or writers themselves. This modernist "coming to writing" topos is manifest in female *Künstlerroman* variations of the genre

    Mandei-lhe uma Boca and *Sara* both adapt the *Bildungroman/ Künstlerroman* formats to the sociological preoccupations which were central to Gonçalves's earlier and better-known testimonial novels, *Floresta em Bremerhaven* and *Ora Esguardae* (Graciete Besse 29-49). By electing to represent an individual woman's coming to writing, Gonçalves tellingly moves away from the polyphonic montage, the dramatically testimonialized voice of the people as multiple, which famously characterized *Ora Esguardae.*[4] The chorus of the "povo" as a unison that fragments, is here replaced by the reintegrated subjectivity of the first person confessional mode, the individual constructed through a series of encounters and relationships. As Abel et al. have remarked, the "individual's relation to society [is] an interaction fundamental to the [*Bildungsroman*] genre" (5). Gonçalves's focus has visibly shifted in these two novels from the impossible fiction of the collective, to the experience of the middle-class individual giving voice to a social conscience.

    In *Mandei-lhe uma Boca* the single voice manifests the immediacy of an oral discourse trying to keep up with the pace of post-revolutionary change manifest in language. *Sara* also retains certain "marcas de oralidade, de gírias [...] ou de calão (às vezes grosseiro)" (122) as Paula Morão notes, but these are

[4] On *Ora Esguardae*, see Ferreira 1989 and Owen 1992.

transposed into the more analytical mode of the 1980s and framed as a metafictionalized "pseudo-autobiography" based on Sara's diaries and reflecting on events at a double remove.[1] In the italicized introduction, a third person narrative voice describes Sara deciding to gather together the diary pages she has kept in an old trunk and to begin editing them for publication. She writes, "a selecção estava feita. E as alterações que se propusera" (9). The dates of chronological sequencing are removed from the diary entries and Sara's social commentaries are ordered according to the narrative logic of a personal growth trajectory, so that the dominant narrative structure remains that of the *Bildungsroman/Künstlerroman*. The social focus of Gonçalves's testimonial work returns then only as the necessary interactive context for the heroine's personal progress. The polyphonic chorus of different voices which spoke the revolution in *Ora Esguardae,* is here mediated by Sara's attempts to reformulate these various registers of language as her own and to demonstrate through reference to formerly taboo subjects, the freedom of speech and dialogue which the revolution has made possible.[2]

Sara initiates her literary apprenticeship with *Mandei-lhe uma Boca* in the specifically liberating context of the "divorce boom" and the destabilization of the family which ensued when the Vatican Concordat was revoked in 1975

---

[1] Graciete Besse, commenting on the text's relationship to the diary format, has aptly described it as, "um discurso organizado segundo uma certa lógica, concentrado em torno do ponto de vista do 'eu' íntimo e das suas incursões no exterior quotidiano ou no seu interior reflexivo, mas sem referência à cronologia" (43).

[2] The attempt to incorporate various registers of language has been the main source of criticism directed at *Sara*. Paula Morão, for example, remarks on the uneven attempt to integrate the various contemporary sociolects of Lisbon youth with Sara's internal, philosophical reflections. She writes, "estes intervalos entre as zonas de pensamento e de linguagem da personagem mostram as dificuldades de realmente entrar no mundo que o livro quer retratar" (122). Luiz Fagundes Duarte, in contrast, defends precisely this aspect of Gonçalves's poetics as "a representação da incongruência e da inverosimilhança que são atributos desta personagem" (1988, 8). Interestingly, in this context, Duarte reads Gonçalves's perceived grounding in realism as a welcome move beyond "aqueles orgasmos palavrosos que certas instâncias – autores, críticos, editores – nos têm impingido como representantes de escrita feminina" (1986, 29).

(Ferreira, V. 174). Riva becomes simultaneously surrogate mother and mentor as Sara discovers that both of her parents are cheating on each other. Where the double standard always protected men whose infidelities were accepted, society is suddenly forced to confront the new sexual freedoms of women, seen here from the disoriented perspective of the daughter rather than the mother. The social hypocrisy surrounding clandestine sexual misdemeanour provides Sara's initiation into the world of mimesis as she becomes aware that the whole of the society in which she lives is a hypocritical work of fiction, deception and performance. She is ironically not aware, however, that her own plan to expose her grandfather's clandestine enjoyment of lovers would implicate her in a similar act of duplicity, if she pursued her idea of tricking him by disguising herself as one of his women. She believes that if her grandfather were unmasked, "talvez se deixasse de pregar moral" (81). Like *Lazarillo de Tormes*, the classic *Bildungsroman* to which Sara refers at the end of the novel, she learns the art of fictional representation through her experience of "appearance" and "reality" in society without being fully aware of her own complicity in the mimetic process as she speaks. However, while Sara identifies strongly with Lazarillo's awakening repeating, "pareció me que en aquel instante desperté de la simpleza en que como niño dormido estaba" (114) she rejects as archetypally masculine the adult Lázaro's model of maturity and social integration as she says "sempre a mesma treta! Os homens!" (114).

The progress of Sara's apprenticeship in art and/as society is indicated through Riva's implied responses to her opinions as she raises Sara's awareness of what the revolution and decolonization meant. For example, Sara has no understanding of the plight of the *retornados* who she blames for unemployment and housing shortages, retorting "ora bolas para a descolonização" (81) when Riva disagrees with her. However, Sara's social integration is significantly mediated by a role model and mentor who lives an alternative, unconventional life on the margins of mainstream, bourgeois society. A liberal product of the 1960s and '70s, Riva writes, lives alone, avoids formal occasions and has been influenced by her time in England. Fernanda Silva-Brummel significantly emphasizes Riva's years in England as the formative influence on her rejection of feminine social conditioning in Portugal. She writes:

> In England studiert sie gemäss ihren geistigen and kulturellen Interessen, finanziert ihr Studium mit eigener Arbeit and bildet sich für ein Berufsleben aus, in dem sie ihre Verwirklichung findet. Riva übernimmt die Verantwortung für sich und für ihre Zukunft. Nach ihrer Rückkehr nach Portugal zahlt sie für ihre mutige Entscheidung jedoch einen hohen Preis. Sie ist der portugiesischen Gesellschaft eine Generation voraus. (135)

> In England she mainly studies her intellectual and cultural interests, finances her studies by working herself and gets an education for a professional life in which she finds her (self) realization. Riva takes responsibility for herself and her future. After her return to Portugal she pays a high price for her courageous decision. She is a generation out of step with Portuguese society. (my translation)

Although the English connection is part of Riva's attraction, Sara stands at a greater temporal and spatial remove from the social context which influenced Riva's self-discovery and this leaves Sara potentially even more culturally and intellectually alienated from her own environment.

Sara's turn inward to reflection and self-analysis is conveyed through her recollections of dreams, fantasies and nightmares (Graciete Besse 31-2). The most significant of these fantasies is inspired by a brief, idealized relationship with Diogo, marking the only exception to her growing cynicism about love, sex and family relations. She spends an afternoon by the sea with him towards the end of *Mandei-lhe uma Boca* and the memory of the occasion stays with her for years, repeatedly recurring as a *leitmotif* in *Sara* connoting other, seemingly lost, opportunities throughout her life. Annis Pratt's analysis of the female novel of development has noted the common topos of young women retreating from an unacceptable social reality into an idyllic, often imagined, love affair which continues into adulthood and becomes a focus of longing and nostalgia. Pratt remarks, "the young woman turns away from 'inappropriate' males towards fantasies of a figure, projected from within her own personality, more suitable to her needs" (22). All of Sara's real relationships with men have been disastrous, as the catalogue of experience she narrates to Riva indicates. Even though Diogo is a "real" entity, their actual encounter is minimal and Sara's enduring fantasy image of him as her only significant love relationship is contingent on his sudden departure and absence from her life. This formative emotional experience marks her withdrawal from the world and her initiation into a therapeutic realm of imagination and fantasy, which will be taken up again in *Sara*, providing the most significant thematic link between the two novels.

Sara records the heroine's more rational, adult judgements on the uneven fabric of Portuguese society which emerged during the transitional period of the 1980s, providing a testimony to the gender-related effects of the social "inconsistencies, disjunctures, or discrepancies" (1997, 34) to which de Sousa Santos referred above. Sara writes of her own generation and the next, "nem eles nem nós, os de vinte-e-tal, guardamos marcas da Pide ou da guerra das colónias. Da Censura. Das perseguições e do medo" (34). The radical breakdown of the family, which was feared in *Mandei-lhe uma Boca*, has not actually taken place eight years later in so far as the hypocrisy of maintaining a unified household continues to hold sway. Sara's mother remains unfaithful to her father, however, and the servant Cândida is still the domestic mainstay of the household. Riva and her younger partner Lauro provide Sara with inspirational models of adulthood as an alternative to her own dysfunctional family with whom she is living while she finishes her degree. As Sara contemplates her future, her career and her relationships, her problem is the proliferation of new choices and opportunities for women in a society not wholly attuned to accommodating the broader social consequences of those choices, as her boyfriend Guilherme's ultimately traditionalist attitudes indicate. As Sara writes of herself, "há muito tempo me encontro de costas para o passado, mas desconheço a forma de articular os gestos que me permitam o futuro" (130).

If the 1970s was the decade of revolutionary fervour and leftist disappointment, the 1980s with its rising capitalist consumerism and growing economy is the time of future shock. Indeed a feature which distinguishes *Sara* from other female *Bildungsromane*, such as those which Labovitz discusses in

English, French and German (255-6) is the lack of any distinct focus for rebellion against bourgeois parents through commitment to political causes and social protests. This was the domain *par excellence* of the generation Sara is rebelling against. The emergence of new religious and political trends is shown drawing Portugal into more conspicuously globalized networks, with fashionable new-age spiritual movements and faiths such as "o ioga, o tauísmo, o budismo zen, o vandantismo, o tantrismo tibetano" (27-8) and the introduction of ecological politics. The old cooperative communes such as that which Lauro tried to establish in the Alentejo during the land occupations have failed or fizzled out, riven by internal rivalry, exhausted idealism and drugs (123-29). Sara jokingly refers to students in France revising the Marseillaise "Allons enfants de l'apathie" (14). Youth seek their inspiration in differently articulated political causes. World revolution has given way to saving the environment, as evidenced by the young people Sara observes undertaking voluntary archeological work on Ilha do Pessegueiro. Defending the post-ideology generation Sara contests the popular 1980s press clichés and stereotypical criticisms of youth declaring:

> Leio o que escrevem sobre a juventude abalada do após Abril. Que a mesma juventude se encontra alienada, grande parte socialmente desinserida, a comunicação perdendo força. E o terror do movimento niilista dos punks. E os conflitos com o patriarcado familiar. Fim de citação! (13)

Sara's response to current media images and her incorporation of the ideolects of her historical moment and social milieu, testify to the new generation's access to a freedom of language and expression, particularly as regards sexuality and the body, which is almost performatively over-indulged in the discourse of the novel. Sara details the frenzied variety of sexual experiences, which she and her friends explore, essaying bisexual and homosexual options as experimental novelties rather than affirmations of identity. Running counter to this liberated climate, the sexual double standard still remains in force and the lack of legal abortion leaves women at the heart of a massive social contradiction, which Sara experiences directly with her own illegal termination. Many of Sara's group no longer rigidly subscribe to the sexual exclusivity of marriage for life, but she tellingly denounces the conservatism of the younger women she knows who timidly reinforce the norms around virginity and marriage which had been all too briefly placed in question. Predicting that the next generation after her own will mark a reactionary, nostalgic return to social tradition, Sara perceives herself as belonging to "uma geração que se assume sem referências, o fim da geração de Sessenta, para o qual o básico pode constituir essa mesma perda de referências" (34).

Sara's historical and geopolitical disorientation is compounded artistically by the dearth of canonical models for the woman writer and the woman philosopher. In her quest for new cultural identifications and inspirations Sara is compelled to discard previous models as part of the process of forging new ones. The inadequacy of the hero or heroine's formal education and the conflict this produces forms a common theme in male and female *Bildungromane* (Labovitz 3-4, 96-7). While Sara admires the fathers of western philosophy from Plato and the Greeks down to Hegel, she is forced to conclude:

> Mas estão longe. Não posso caminhar ao lado deles, reencontrá-los. [...] Como iniciada da Filosofia, sinto-me pobre, sem estímulo. Queria esquecer. Correntes filosóficas, e arquétipos literários, e padrões de cultura. (154)

She is more inspired by the idea of making a short intimate film of two hands in dialogue, voicing her experience of the world somatically as "um lugar de calor, um elo entre nós e os outros, [que] seria um lugar-mãe" (154).

Sara's attempt to inscribe herself into a literary discourse of her own is related to her quest for this "lugar-mãe", the search for the genealogical antecedent, the missing mother, in literature and in life. Where *Mandei-lhe uma Boca* had boldly declared Sara's intention to discard the outmoded, hypocritical family, *Sara* moves to reconcile the broken relationships of the 1970s and to trace her identity through her recent ancestry. In the process of discovering herself, Sara records the impact of recent historical changes on three generations of women within, or connected to, her own family. Sara's mother, Tia Salette and Riva convey the conflicts of the previous generation which countered the strictures of Salazarism with a combination of complicity, submission and passive resistance. A more uniform, unchallenging acceptance of the patriarchal Catholic *status quo* is evinced by the generation of her grandmother, Alcina the bailiff's wife, and the longstanding family servant, Cândida. Neither Sara's mother nor her grandmother offers a role model for behaviour that is relevant to Sara's own generation. Rather they occupy two extreme poles with regard to marriage, family and sexual relations. The former is scandalously adulterous, and the latter is rigidly faithful. Sara's mother has an affair with Jorge, a man closer to her daughters' age and to whom Rosário had also been attracted. Sara's father is a Freudian psychoanalyst whose profession affords a highly ironical perspective on the dysfunctional state of his own family. The oedipalized Freudian family has replaced the Holy Family as Sara's intellectual referent for modern family analysis and she mockingly refers to psychotherapy as the new religious confessional.

The opposite extreme of Sara's mother sexual self-indulgence is provided by Tia Salette who, during the Salazar years, had suppressed the real passion of her life for the benefit of an advantageous marriage, only to meet her first love again and regret her abstinence many years later. The secret revelations of this outwardly conformist and sexually proper generation form the focus of a still clandestine feminine world for Sara and her peers. The private, subtextual conversation between aunt and niece is interrupted and suspended when Sara's father joins them with banal interventions about weather and petrol prices, only for the women's confidences to be avidly resumed as soon as he leaves the room. A covert, unspecified sense of complicity with other women, and a need to understand their past, has replaced any explicit sense of political identification or female solidarity for Sara, engaged in a less clearly defined struggle under more diffuse modern conditions. Sara thinks:

> A geração da tia Salette soube de uma religião e duma
> sociedade autoritárias e opressivas. Por isso a geração de
> Sessenta foi revolucionária. A de Setenta uma geração
> vencida. E a nossa está impotente, desencantada, está numa
> grande confusão. Mas insurgindo-se. Nem sempre
> energicamente, mas insurgindo-se. (56)

Tia Salette and Sara's mother are both perceived as victims in ways which
Sara and her sister Rosário choose not to emulate as they make a radical break
with the hegemony of marriage. Sara refuses a proposal of marriage from
Guilherme. Rosário is driven by the discovery of the mother's affair to leave the
family home and seek her fortunes in Paris where she enters a relationship with a
French woman, Claudine (50-1). Rosário has a series of close "friendships" with
other women, never overtly named as lesbian, but implied as such when Sara
elliptically describes Rosário's first night in bed with Claudine, "foi mais ou
menos assim que mo contou. Mais ou menos assim" (50). In contrast to the fierce
rivalries and hostilities between female relations, trapped and isolated by the
patriarchal sexual economy in *Novas Cartas*, *Sara* provides strong images of
union, protection, acceptance and reconciliation between the women of Sara's
family, as she grows gradually closer to Rosário and ultimately forgives her
mother. However, whilst Sara learns to understand her mother's failings and
insecurities, their relationship is characterized by a series of disencounters,
symptomatic of the temporary disjuncture in historical patterns of family
continuity. Maria Luisa Nunes's description of this aspect of *Mandei-lhe uma
Boca* is, if anything, even more applicable to *Sara*, as she refers to "an adolescent
female in search of a mother, and the generation of the mother bereft of the old
values and myths that gave meaning to life" (26).

In the absence of support from her mother Sara turns to her grandmother
for inspiration. She perceives her grandmother as belonging to a mythical world
of superstition and fatalism in which "falava ainda dos prurídos, de tormentos, de
martírios, de desonras para o lar, do fado de certas famílias, de ânsias
infinitas...da carne ser fraca (140). Cândida, the servant who has raised Sara,
similarly represents a dying breed since 1974, a model of traditional obedience
and self-sacrifice horrified at the lack of respect shown by the new breed of
domestics. During a spectacular quarrel with the younger, free-thinking servant
Dores, Cândida is comically double-voiced by her misuse of the word "cravo" to
mean "escravo", describing her own mother as "um cravo perfeito" (19) who
raised fifteen children. To this, Dores retorts "um cravo perfeito? Ó senhora

Cândida, cravos só os do 25, que eu até gosto deles, mas a sua mãe viveu longe destes tempos" (19). The lives of women like Cândida's mother are typified by the figure of Alcina, the wife of the "feitor" at the family estate near Porto, who leads such a brutalized existence that Sara is angered by her passivity (69).

Despite the double generation gap separating their beliefs Sara's grandmother and Cândida afford the continuity which she is seeking to re-establish. The outmoded historical wisdom which Sara's grandmother possessed is effectively revalidated when she reinforces her links with her female ancestry and inserts her story into an ongoing history of women. The transgenerational connection between women is reinforced through symbolic gifts such as the grandmother's garnet ring and the heirloom shawl which Cândida gives to Sara. The gift which Sara offers Cândida in return is her ability to record Cândida's life for posterity in the act of writing, the ultimate magical gift which Riva will eventually pass on to Sara with the words "'a escrita já está contigo'[....] 'Tens só de acreditar no próximo instante'" (97).

Sara increasingly derives solace, escape and a belief in the future from a woman-centred literary environment as her relationships with men prove unsatisfying. Her boyfriend Guilherme is an updated version of the maritime discoverer, an airline pilot, who uses travel to acquire the latest luxury consumer goods and to spice up his life through exotic relationships. Sara realizes that women have changed and men have not culturally caught up with them. Guilherme remarks that his ideal women are those he met in Malaysia to which Sara retorts, "o de mãe-serva, não. O de mãe-serva constitui um número acabado, repouse em paz (20). Sara breaks her addiction to her purely sexual relationship with Guilherme and resists the biological blackmail of marrying for children fully aware that she has taken a decisive maturing step as she thinks, "será assim que se envelhece" (165). The heroine's decision regarding marriage is commonly the turning point in female *Bildung*. Sara's refusal of marriage conditions her adult identity by clearing the way for Diogo, the idealized lover of her adolescence, to return and ultimately precipitating the longstanding inclination to be a writer which had first been mooted in *Mandei-lhe uma Boca.*

Diogo is a sensitive trainee architect who seems to be the opposite of Guilherme's sexual voracity and crass materialism. Echoing Pratt's description of the lovers which *Bildungsroman* heroines tend to imagine, the adult Diogo no longer corresponds to the fantasized recollections of him which Sara had retained from her teenage memory over the past eight years. As Pratt remarks, this nostalgic mental escapism "calls up from the feminine unconscious the image of an ideal lover and almost always includes a rejection of social expectation concerning engagement and marriage" (23). Sara's dreams of Diogo are effectively bound up with leaving behind the prospect of marriage in Portugal, travelling to Italy with him and fulfilling her artistic aspiration as she declares her love for "as Artes! Terra amante!. Um chão que nos pode dar tudo, entre a voz forrada de chuva, o longo olhar dos deuses, e a nossa medida" (195). She imagines following in the footsteps of great writers, the reference to Goethe emphasizing the proximity of her fictional project to the roots of the Romantic *Bildungsroman* tradition. She tries, through Diogo's descriptions, to picture herself walking through Vicenza to the spot where "Goethe caminhou no seu primeiro encontro com a cidade" (182).

In an updating of the original fantasy the adult Diogo who has returned to Lisbon begins to correspond to Sara's revised blueprint of an ideal partner. However, as Pratt observes:

> The ideal lover is sometimes embodied in real men during erotic epiphanies in women's fiction, but such experiences are momentary and fleeting, giving way to events that act as punishments. (24)

Sara is effectively "punished" for her aspirations when Diogo disappears again without explanation as suddenly as he had come and she discovers he has a girlfriend Stefania, who is pregnant by him, and requires his immediate return to Italy. Following his departure, it is to Riva that Sara confides her intention of transposing her negative experience into art by producing a novel. One of her inspirational models, in contrast to Goethe or *Lazarillo de Tormes*, is *The Color Purple* the popular 1980s African-American *Bildungsroman* by Alice Walker which Sara has read and cites in English. This inspiration combined with Riva's encouragement leads her to edit and publish a novel constructed from the last four years of her diaries.

The competing pressures on Sara, however, result in a split between her social and artistic identifications formally manifested in her dilemma concerning the selection of an appropriate conclusion for her novel (Pratt 35). Ambivalent endings constitute a common feature of the feminine *Bildungsroman* genre where women's development is contextually circumscribed (Labovitz 6). The romantic aesthetic impulse towards closure suggested by the need for completed adult development in the *Bildungsroman*, conflicts with the vestigially sociological, testimonial frame of reference in which Sara has defined herself and within which her choices are still relatively limited. The result is a retreat from social and historical "reality" discourses in favour of asserting the individual artistic ego, the creative (male) subject of romantic and modernist traditions, as Riva encourages Sara to make a distinction between autobiography and fiction. The result of this in *Sara* is the conspicuous relinquishing of historical referencing and a double conclusion. Olga Gonçalves herself gives the following insight into this aspect of the novel:

> Sara fala com Riva e mostra o seu desapontamento pela existência de Stefania e pela súbita partida de Diogo para Vicenza. Ela decidira escrever uma autobiografia, e sabia-lhe mal terminá-la desse modo. Pesava-lhe a sua própria imagem num campo de abandono. E Riva aponta-lhe o valor da transfiguração, as múltiplas possibilidades que um escritor tem ao seu alcance. (1986a, 5)

Either ending potentially casts Sara and Stefania as phallically divided rivals and both reveal Sara departing in different senses. In the idealized story with Diogo, she literally leaves Portugal for Italy as the romantic inspirational fulfilment of love and art. In the act of writing, she metaphorically departs from a painful and uncertain present seeking the imaginative escape of emotional sublimation in metafiction. Sara's final gesture towards identity is suggestively couched in the figurative language of the voyage as she thinks "estou noutra, a curtir noutra! Por exemplo: ficar numa de coragem, buscar o rumo em que me identifique" (209).

This concluding device is, of course, highly ironic from a feminist *Bildungsroman* perspective. The very narrative act which installs Sara as a writer, also enshrines as fiction her dream of sexual and emotional fulfillment. Diogo may be imagined as the "new" man, the spiritual helpmate and intellectual companion, but the punishing intervention of reality has shown him to be still very much the "old" man, whose travels leave a trail of emotional devastation behind him. Although the ending plays out the fictional scenario of Diogo and Sara in Italy together, the emphasis remains on the continuities of Sara's past. She recalls the turns of a waltz danced by her grandmother half a century ago and finds the lost garnet ring passed down the generations until her grandmother had given it to her. The ring, traditionally a symbol of marriage, acquires here different connotations of creative power and generational legacy between women. Sara uses it to connote a new self-acceptance, a wedding of conflicting elements in a divided self which is ultimately made whole but only through a solipsistic retreat into aesthetics which is also a "deslizar para o abstracto" (210).

The process of *Bildung* is conventionally deemed complete when the heroine achieves "the evolution of a coherent self" (Abel et al. 13). Sara does not, however, bring the new coherent solutions one might have expected, to the classic women's tension between professional and sexual fulfilment, and indeed the stability of her coherence seems undermined when she remarks "não sei o que escrevo" (210). The rather contrived fictional happy ending is, in some respects, a flaw in the novel. The assertion of the romantic, creative ego through unquestioned narrative modalities of genealogy and exclusionary representational poetics is itself complicit in the reinforcement of the conservative socio-symbolic structures which militate against Sara's heteronomous development beyond a set of limited, mutually excluding choices. If the literary equivalent of equal rights feminism means speaking from the place of the masculine *Bildungsroman* narrator and following in the footsteps of Goethe after all, Sara seems ultimately condemned to keep turning within the same narrative circle.

The final novel I will explore, Lídia Jorge's *Notícia da Cidade Silvestre*, is also a historically-focused female *Bildungsroman/Künstlerroman* which engages like *Sara* in the transformation of a testimonial "reality" discourse through the device of a metafictionalized diary. Emphasizing subjectivity over identity, however, *Notícia* recasts the "woman coming to writing" genre in a nascently postmodern idiom. Continuing the radical displacement of symbolic representational conventions variously broached in *Novas Cartas*, *Paisagem* and *Montedemo*, *Notícia* engages with the ethical question of the woman writer's relationship to mimeticism. Devising new ways to reconcile the intimate and the instrumental Jorge decentres the traditional *Bildungsroman* identity fictions without denying women's material experience as embodied subjects of their own histories.

CHAPTER 5

A Walk on the Wild Side in Lídia Jorge's *Notícia da Cidade*
Silvestre

Três vezes nos trairão/Nossos irmãos: no pão, no corpo/E na
cidade. (Barreno et al. 94)

It is not in the great forests nor on pathways that philosophy is
elaborated, but in the cities and streets, including even their
most *factitious* aspects. (Deleuze 1983, 55-6)

Also in Raissa, city of sadness, there runs an invisible thread
that binds one living being to another for a moment, then
unravels, then is stretched again between moving points as it
draws new and rapid patterns so that at every second an
unhappy city contains a happy city unaware of its own
existence. (Calvino 137)

Notícia da Cidade Silvestre, Lídia Jorge's third novel, was published in 1984.
Written from a first person feminine perspective, it follows the lives of two
women struggling to survive in the economic and demographic chaos of Lisbon
in the post-revolutionary period of 1975-9. Like most of the women writers who
emerged in Portugal in the 1980s, Jorge has tended to be equivocal about feminist
critical readings *per se*, reacting to the perceived threat of a gendered literary
aesthetics.[1] In 1983 for example, she writes "o artista perfeito é aquele que,

---

[1] In a 1985 interview with Júlio Pinto for *Diário de Notícias* Jorge praises the pioneering
work of the Three Marias and regrets that in many ways the feminism of the 1970s "não foi tão

sendo homem, adivinha o mais possível o que se passa nas mulheres e, sendo mulher, tem a percepção do que se passa nos homens. A qualidade estética é supra-sexual" (Louro 1983, 27).[2] Notwithstanding the erasure of power differentials which the aesthetic ideal of androgyny can tend to imply, an awareness of the historical need for the reclamation of women's voice and space in Portuguese letters has figured prominently in Jorge's interviews over the years. She has referred to the significance of the Three Marias in particular as forerunners of the present generation of women writers in Portugal:

> Por outro lado, também somos beneficiados pelo facto de ter havido movimentos de mulheres mais velhas que nós (caso das 'Novas Cartas Portuguesas'), o que, de certa forma, acabou por nos dar um passaporte de igualdade no domínio da escrita. (Louro 1983, 26)

Writing in the spaces which this "passport of equality" deterritorialized for women writers, *Notícia da Cidade Silvestre* more than any of the works previously discussed here, picks up on the Three Marias' engendering of Portugal's shifting national identifications in relation to the end of imperialism. Positing a half real, half fantasy metropolis somewhere between point of return and point of departure, *Notícia* moves to reinvent "the City" as no longer the locus of imperial power or as she herself expresses it "a sintomatologia da nossa *pequeninidade*, enquanto corpo colectivo" (1986, 58).[3] Echoing, or rather

---

longe quanto deveria ter ido" (6). However, in tune with the post-Marxist, post-ideology climate of the 1980s she concludes in post-feminist mood "foi necessário haver feministas, para que agora haja as não-feministas" (5). Jorge has, however, remained a vocal supporter of abortion campaigns. See Jorge 1993, 32 for her criticisms of Pope John Paul II.

[2] Jorge describes Orlando as "um homem que se transforma em mulher e que atravessa três séculos metade do tempo um ser, metade outro, sempre os dois, a figura andrógina, profundamente angélica, que Virginia Woolf sempre procurou" (1989, 32). See also Louro 1983 and 1984 for Jorge's views on gender and writing.

[3] See "Escrita e Emancipação" published in 1986 but written in 1984, the year in which *Notícia* was published, for Jorge's own evaluation of cultural and social changes effecting the production of literature a decade after the revolution. See also Sapega 1997 for discussion of *A Costa dos Murmúrios* in terms of "national reterritorialization" (181).

anticipating, her more famous critique of colonial historicist epistemologies in *A Costa dos Murmúrios* (1988) Jorge makes a gendered point of entry to the subject focusing on women's relationships to power and violence, representation and the other. In interview in 1985 Jorge remarked:

> O que acontece é que o nosso poder é subversivo, por um lado, e é escondido, por outro.... E eu não sei até que ponto as guerras têm sido feitas, as lutas, as descobertas, não têm sido impulsionadas por rostos femininos. Por alguma coisa as mulheres têm deixado que o Poder tenha sempre esse rosto masculino.... Talvez tenha sido também cómodo, para as mulheres. (Pinto, J. 6)

A Costa dos Murmúrios positions the interdependent figures of Eva Lopo and Helena de Tróia in asymmetrical dialogue. *Notícia da Cidade Silvestre* is superficially similar in that it is built around a conflicted relationship between two women, Anabela Dias Cravo and Júlia Grei. Their lives typify the late 1970s climate of social and political instability and family breakdown. Júlia Grei is the widow of David Grei, a former sculptor and anti-fascist *resistente*. She has a small boy, João Mário, who is nicknamed Jóia. Neither Júlia nor Anabela fits the traditional family model which had been central to Estado Novo society, since the former's husband has died and the latter has rejected family life in favour of pursuing a career in the male-dominated legal profession. Initially, they provide an uneasy, sporadic source of support for each other but Anabela begins to assume an overweening power over Júlia's life, conspicuously occupying the dominant masculine provider role in relation to Júlia's timid self-abnegation. Júlia lives cooped up in the damp sculpture workshop of her dead husband and earns a meagre living in a bookshop owned by Sr. Assumpção who is attracted to her. She also sews and sells rag dolls to make ends meet. Anabela's strategy for getting on in life centres around relationships with her "padrinho", with her various bosses, Atouguia Ferraz and Baptista Falcão, and with a host of different men as material needs dictate.

The political and economic circumstances of the post-revolutionary period dictate an extensive realignment of the old manicheisms of (anti-)fascism, which condition Júlia's and Anabela's negotiations with power. The small traumas and insignificant battles of the women's individual lives are played out in relation to the common social themes associated with the end of the revolutionary crisis, the collapse of the communist ascendancy, and the rise of commercial capitalism under the new democracy. The old hard left are shown to be disorientated by defeat - as symbolized by the death of David Grei himself - or betraying their old values and cashing in on the new opportunities. Traditional social attitudes and hierarchies return surreptitiously to find slightly updated forms and interpretations as Sr. Assumpção implies when he comments, "meus amigos, não há diferença nenhuma - só a ditadura era um tempo demasiado lento, e a democracia um tempo demasiado rápido" (251). From the women's point of view, the men in this post-revolutionary distopia still govern access to money, employment, legal rights and sexual gratification and the women are expected to act in Jorge's words as "'ventríloquas dos homens'" (Almeida Martins 10). Increased sexual freedom remains bound by cultural and legal conservatism on issues such as abortion. Maria Teresa Horta describes *Notícia* as a novel "onde as mulheres se movem numa paisagem assustadora. Tão nossa conhecida" and in which "o contacto entre elas se dá, a um nível diverso dos homens - do relacionamento entre os homens" (1984, 11). However, in a radical break with the feminine solidarity paradigm of *Novas Cartas*, female friendship does not provide any real solace or protection either as the women's paths diverge, only for them to meet in the violent encounter of the conclusion. When Júlia is summarily dropped by Anabela and becomes estranged from her, she tries to outdo Anabela at her own game, cynically reducing relationships to physical pleasure and material gain or as she puts it "agarrada só ao meu corpo" (273).

Beyond the recognizable social turmoil of the post-revolution, however, the third person narrator who frames the novel refers to a significant non-happening, or a non-moment in History when s/he remarks that there does not appear to have been a cataclysm such as a war in the city. Evoking the years 1975-1979 paradoxically as a remembered lacuna of memory the narrator writes "ninguém se lembra de ter passado nenhuma guerra, nenhuma fome, nem sequer nenhuma epidemia" (15). The geographically distant non-remembered Colonial

War has given way to a decolonization process which seems ostensibly relevant to the novel only in so far as it is the actual, or perceived, reason for acute housing shortages and racial tensions. The empire has come home to roost only to find no home to roost in. Urban overcrowding has ensued on a large scale following the influx of demobilized soldiers, wounded veterans, *retornados*, and black immigrants from the former colonies. Anabela's "padrinho" complains of a "vivenda" being given to "um batalhão de pessoas vindas duma colónia qualquer, quatro ou cinco famílias que lá viviam engalfinhadas e até ameaçavam destruir os marmeleiros" (59). The *retornados* and new black immigrants bear the brunt of people's frustrations. Júlia's trade as a prostitute is interrupted when an innocent Cabo-Verdiano immigrant is knifed by a drunk (286).

The Lisbon locations which Júlia and Anabela inhabit and the street names to which they refer are a constant reminder of a now superseded imperial era commemorated in cement and stone, the Praça do Império (16) and the Bairro das Colónias (121). If the metropolis is suddenly the new home of the returning "empire", the nation also finds itself newly positioned in the global order as "a democracia consolidava a sua franjinha radicular dentro de água" (15-16). The national borders have shrunk, the sea no longer looks beyond, rather it delimits and confines within. The great port of departure is now more a port of entry for the new people and goods pouring into the country. In the mid-1970s the docks were notoriously hazardous for pedestrians "porque descarregavam dos barcos caixas de pau cheias de haveres mínimos e máximos de gente que abandonava África" (93). Reflecting increasing relations with the capitalist west and the USA, the old Bar Aviador becomes the Together/Tonight. The ships observed by Jóia do not contain cameras and special espionage pens that conceal guns, as he had fancifully imagined. Rather, they are responding to the new domestic consumer goods boom as Júlia remarks, "agora tudo o que entrava e saía era pacífico, electrodoméstico" (20).

The disjunctures arising from the shift in world position are transposed onto the cultural and linguistic plane when Júlia tries to summarize her "trial by fire" with a quotation for which she cannot identify the source. The narrator traces it to William Carlos Williams repeating, "arregaçai as fimbrias dos vossos mantos, minhas senhoras, para não se queimarem: vamos atravessar o Inferno" (15). However, as V. points out, the quote does not sound the same in Portuguese, "esta língua bárbara que de longe se assemelha à dos velhos mujiques magoados com o seu senhor, o que é bem diferente" (15). The experiences of Portugal, and its "língua bárbara" are resistant to mediation through the cultural hegemony of anglophone America. The Portuguese language sounds at a distance like Russian peasants bemoaning their oppression. Trapped on the edges of Europe, Portugal is marginal to the USA, the USSR and the conflicts of the Cold War. Nor does recourse to the classical roots of Greek antiquity offer a stable connection to the past. The Greek language, which legendarily gave the city of Lisbon its name derived from Ulysses, is invoked here only to underline the irrelevance of such a fact in a changing world order. At the beginning of the novel, Júlia observes a white ship on the river bearing an indecipherable Greek name, which she writes down on the hem of her skirt and takes to the bookshop owner Sr. Assumpção to translate. The words "Panta rei" mean "Tudo muda" (15) a common catch phrase of the transition constantly placed in question throughout the novel. The repressed and muted signs of decolonization set against the "changeless" architecture of the city seem to form no more than the details of a historically indexed *mise en scène*. Yet the symbolisms of the imperial order are destined to keep returning against the erasure of amnesia, figuratively inflecting the narrative of transformation, the *Bildungsroman* as historical allegory, which ostensibly structures the novel.

In the tradition of the *Bildungsroman* Júlia grows in awareness through bitter experience of life.[4] When Jóia makes an unsuccessful suicide attempt with rat poison in chapter 33 of the novel, Júlia is forced to recognize that she cannot easily imitate Anabela's aggressively acquisitive lifestyle because of her responsibility to her son. The poisoning triggers the personal crisis described in Júlia's italicized diary entries, which punctuate the chapters of the "novel" itself

---

[4] See Gaspar Simões for a suggestive reading of *Notícia* as picaresque with Anabela Cravo as Portugal's only "pícaro nacional" (31).

and install the *Bildungsroman/Künstlerroman* topos of the woman coming to writing. This metafictional device affords a split perspective, a questioning of memory, which reveals the suppressions and omissions of mimeticism.[5] Although it is primarily focalized by Júlia in the first person, the novel opens with the voice of a third person extradiegetic narrator, whom Júlia will address somewhat anachronistically as V. suggesting an abbreviation of Vossa Senhoria or Vossa Mercê. The gender and identity of V. are never specified, recalling perhaps Jorge's ideal androgynous narrator, and V. claims to have met Júlia in unusual circumstances, noticing her from the window of the "Bar Together/Tonight". Júlia's desire to sell her diaries has drawn V. to find her again as the latter explains, "foi esse insólito numa terra destas que me fez voltar a procurá-la, achando que bem podia Júlia Grei alinhavar a lembrança com alguma ordem e mais algum proveito" (16-17). Having come into possession of Júlia's diary, the "caderno de capa amarela", as well as her more randomly scribbled notes or "papéis", V. has then been instrumental in converting these fragments into a novel, though it is never fully explained how.[6] When Júlia prepares to part company with V. at the end she writes "foi bom que tivesse mediado este tempo de penumbra" (308) referring to the events described in the novel as an indeterminate, interstitial between-space. A clear allegorical resonance here is the "tempo 'suspenso'" between "historicidade individual e colectiva" with which Maria de Lourdes Pintasilgo characterizes the period (1986, 66).

The diaries are ultimately less important and occupy less space in the finished product than the random "papéis que me ia mandando pelo correio, ou por quem calhava" (17). The two sources operate out of synchrony as the diary

---

[5] My thanks are due to Paula Jordão for sharing her valuable doctoral research on this aspect of the novel with me.

[6] V. also clearly has access to a world beyond Portugal and a knowledge of other cultures and languages as well as an awareness of the commercial literature market. In this respect it is tempting to read V. as a fictionalized author surrogate, who perceives the need to defend Portuguese cultural specificity against new trends of northern European and North American cultural homogenization. For Jorge's own views on this in 1984 see "Escrita e Emancipação" (1986).

entries referring to Jóia post-date all the chapters up until chapter 33. The diary as a dated, documentary chronicle has been superseded and displaced by the subjective impressions of Júlia's daily experience. She addresses V. directly as implied reader throughout and even when it is indicated that V. has missed some of their encounters (176, 199) s/he continues to function therapeutically in the mode of analyst/confessor. In the "papéis" Júlia has more overt recourse to fiction and fantasy, as she states in various formulations throughout the novel, "por incrível que [lhe] pareça" (21, 50, 166, 192, 240, 243, 253, 296, 314, 322) measuring the distance travelled from the now barely believable events she is retrospectively describing. In the manner of the early chronicles of maritime travel and "discovery", her powers of description must rise to the challenge of charting for the reader the "prodigious events" of a world they cannot see and therefore may not believe. The limits of mimeticism are drawn in the author's epigraph from a poem by José Martí the father of Cuban liberation: "mas piensa, público amigo,/Que cuando el alma se espanta/Y se tiene en la garganta/Fiero dogal por testigo,/La inteligencia se abrasa/Y el alma se empequeñece,/Y cuanto escribe parece/Obra mezquina y escasa.[7]

In the face of unrepresentable somatic experience, Júlia Grei's "testemunho" is freely reproduced as "uma espécie de intimidade falada" (11), the intimation of physical proximity and the tracing of affect, rather than the myth of readerly identification with represented suffering. As such, the work marks the beginning of a generic transition from the confident assertions of testimonial to the postmodernist mode of historiographic metafiction.[8] As Ana Paula Ferreira has remarked in her reading of Jorge's *A Instrumentalina*:

[7] The Martí phrase "y el alma se empequeñece" also reorientates the famous line from Fernando Pessoa's "Mar Português", "tudo vale a pena/se a alma não é pequena" often taken to support the sacrificial imperative of the maritime expansion. The phrase "vale a pena" recurs throughout *Notícia* by way of questioning the cost of new social, material and sexual values.

[8] I adopt Linda Hutcheon's succinct and useful definition of the term historiographic metafiction as referring to novels which "both install and then blur the line between fiction and history" (113). See her chapter on "Historiographic Metafiction: 'The Pastime of Past Time'" 105-123

> Oscillating between the questioning of any truth claim bearing
> the imprint of the metaphysical, humanist logos and a renewed
> political and ethical imperative of referentials, Jorge's fictions,
> somewhere between John Dewey's philosophy of
> "instrumentalism" and Richard Rorty's "pragmatism," put into
> play ideas as tools for living within a postmodern episteme
> (99).

The necessary referents of post-revolution and post-empire punctuate the diffused, anti-representational poetics of *Notícia*, apparently displacing the tropes of (masculine) rationalism which underpinned the defunct discourse of empire only for these tropes to return, as Jorge implies, in the exploitative capitalist consumerism of the new democratic order. The renaissance vision of the cosmos, the great chain of being and the fixed and regulated spaces of the universe are placed in creative flux. The model of a globe "em pequeno volume" (Camões 336) the centre of the anachronistically Ptolemaic universe shown to Vasco da Gama in Canto X of *Os Lusíadas* reappears in ironic, postmodern mode as the unbelievably kitsch drinks cabinet which Júlia knows will appeal to Saraiva, a former colonial soldier. She offers him:

> Um poderoso globo, suspenso das hastes duma esfera celeste,
> em lindas cores amarelas e esverdinhadas, lembrando os
> tempos da circum-navegação, dos astrolábios, sextantes e rotas
> de marear. Com o toque de pé, porém, a representação da
> Terra abria e de dentro descobriam-se três garrafas de uísque
> com os seus também poderosos copos de friso doirado. (301-2)

By scaling the concept of a Ptolemaically-centred Portugal down to more appropriate proportions *Notícia* charts the implosion of empire as the reconceptualization of aesthetics. Fernando Rita, for example, sculpts a new Eden of flowers, fruit and vegetables to ornament a peaceful universe but he significantly and realistically substitutes "coisa" for cosmos, telling Júlia "'coisa! Cosmos não me diz respeito, é uma grandeza demasiado completa para me fazer feliz. Coisa, digo-te eu'" (160). The "Saber, alto e profundo" which has created Camões's "grande máquina do Mundo" (337) is, as will become evident in *Notícia*, forced into dialogue with an alternative world of "conhecer".

The poetics of the novel, implicitly Júlia's (re)nascent poetics, are characterized by the play of simulacra in a radical move to liberate living bodies as sites of multiple affect from the lapidary representations of an imperial past, too easily recycled in the anachronistic humanist certainties of the present. In his famous essay "Plato and the Simulacrum" the radical philosopher, Gilles Deleuze, recuperates "the false as power" (1983, 53) and raises Platonic "simulacra" to a privileged status precisely because they are corrupted by the fact of their dissemblance.[9] The criteria of resemblance and dissemblance according to which Plato distinguishes good "iconic" copies from false copies or "simulacra" are, as Deleuze affirms, based on inner spiritual resemblance to the Idea of the thing rather than external likenesses. For Deleuze it is because the simulacrum is "constructed around a disparity, a difference; it interiorizes a dissimilitude" (49) that it "includes within itself the differential point of view, and the spectator is made part of the simulacrum, which is transformed and deformed according to his point of view" (49). This internal disparity of the simulacrum becomes a positive dynamic force "which negates both *original and copy, both model and reproduction*" (53) and therefore does not hierarchically install a truth or Ideal as model.

The novel begins with V. as narrator describing the mutability of the human image, the external physical changes in people who buy new clothes or cut their hair. Images are shown to be merely changes of clothing, shifting tricks of light and shade, two-dimensional figures on the film and television screen and, as so often in Jorge's fiction, the effects of masquerade and theatre. Júlia's personal history begins with the need to refashion her world following her sudden transfiguration from a wife to a widow. Her home, which has no windows, is near the mouth of a river "com antemar" and it is here that she waits in the eternal feminine pose of Penelope, not for her husband but for Anabela Cravo to arrive. She recalls her dead husband's assertion that a cry released on one side of the

---

[9] See Ferreira 1999, 99 and 101. Although the play of simulacra is not as intense or pronounced as in later works such as *A Última Dona*, Jorge's pursuit of an anti-humanist poetics is clearly announced in *Notícia*.

river could shatter glass at a considerable distance on the other bank but now "já ninguém precisa bradar" (19). This peaceful new social order, post-war and post-revolution, in which no-one needs to "bradar", is effectively interrogated, however, through a monstrous, alienating trope of disordering in the carnivalesque figure of Anabela Cravo as ersatz man.

Júlia's deceased husband, with his authoritative grasp on epistemology and his old empirical certainties about the distance sound could travel, has been replaced by Anabela, a bizarre imitation of the all-powerful, all-knowing "man" as the new axis for Júlia's androcentric universe. Anabela, unlike Júlia, inhabits and conquers space confidently, as "ela dominava por completo os roteiros e os troços de rua que feitos a pé ligavam cruzamentos e cruzamentos para se chegar mais cedo" (20). She arrives with a rabbit fur jacket draped over her arm, which she casually throws at Júlia the better to impersonate Tarzan, whose cry does not carry over the river, to demonstrate to Júlia that everything her husband had once told her "não passava de fantasia" (22). Anabela thus provides the focus for a critical, because alienated, perspective on still prevalent yet antiquated masculinities as she adopts the postures of a male actor wearing animal skins and impersonating a "savage" in imperialist western film iconography.[10]

This introduction to Anabela as Tarzan, sets the scene for a series of masculine impostures and impersonations throughout the novel which cast Anabela as a grotesque. Since the ironizing gaze which interprets these imitations always belongs to Júlia, they do not empower Anabela, whose performances are unselfconscious and unknowing. The figure of Anabela distraught with grief, for example, defies the established sculptural canon as seen by Júlia who captures images momentarily in ironically displaced relation to the artistic models around her in Grei's sculpture workshop:

> Por aquele barracão tinham passado figuras de cócoras, de pé,
> a cavalo, sentadas, jazidas, cinzentas, brancas, feitas, desfeitas,
> humanóides, zoóides, erectas, retraídas, depostas, como em
> casa de qualquer escultor, bom ou mau não interessa, mas não

[10] I am indebted to Lígia Silva and her doctoral research on *Notícia* for illuminating discussion of this aspect of the novel in relation to the theories of Judith Butler.

me lembrava de nenhuma que se pudesse parecer com a súbita
figura de Anabela Cravo, chorando pelo Atouguia para dentro
do meu colo (104).

As Anabela's statement of excess is derived from Júlia's corrective perception,
the latter's critical descriptions of her in retrospect betray the effects of her
alienation from Anabela and all that she represents. Júlia instructs V./the reader
to note that "Anabela distinguia o fantástico da fantasia" (24). From their
competing conceptualizations of fantasy, their relationship will develop into a
battle for creative primacy over the processes of imitation and invention *per se*.

If Anabela imitates outside appearances as if they were essentially "real",
Júlia asserts her space in the world by exploiting the emptiness of the
simulacrum, starting from the sculptures which Grei has left in the *atelier*. Her
asides to the reader effectively break the mystique of the silent enigmatic woman
as sculptural model in the classical canon. Her cramped conditions force her to
hang her washing over Grei's bronze heads and wooden fish. She thus reshapes
Grei's publically orientated creations by describing the ways in which daily,
intimate domestic life ironizes their intentions, setting up new chains of
association. Her own presence in the *atelier* is marked out by distances and
empty space. For example, when Artur Salema moves her washing and grabs
hold of a pair of her stockings, she recalls "pegou-lhes pelo cós e uma delas
desenrolou-se até ao pé e mostrou-se a baloiçar no ar no feitio duma perna" (30).
Similarly, when asked if she modelled for Grei's Mediterranean-style statue of a
woman she deduces that, because Jóia has painted the statue's nails with a marker
pen and made her look flirtatious, "nenhuma palavra que ela inspirasse como
apropósito me poderia parecer honrosa" (26). Júlia thus comes to occupy the
negative space which delineates the outer contours of represented objects in a
drawing. Speaking from this sculptural "space-off", she exploits her invisibility
to frame others satirically in the "space-on". Mão Dianjo, for example, she
describes in architectural terms as a grotesque, "paralisado por uma espécie de
medo estático, como os desorbitados olhos das gárgulas que escoam as águas dos
mosteiros" (303).

Júlia's most direct encounter with the monumentalization of memory concerns her dead husband's last commission, a stone tribute to the anti-Estado Novo resistance. He has fashioned "a Pomba", with a woman's head and a dove's body. Ambivalently connoting both peace and revolution the "pomba" is significantly "apenas meio liberta" (26).[11] The statue never finds a suitable public space among the "povo" for whom it was created and Grei himself is hit by a car shortly afterwards. Like the grandiose aspirations of the revolution, the statue seems disproportionate and aesthetically incongruous in its settings, a misjudgement of scales and sizes, which people no longer want to celebrate. It resembles an "esfinge em tamanho doméstico" (26), the classic image of the feminine as enigma, here sheltering "uma figura de homem acocorado [que] ora parecia protegido ora derrubado pelas patas, conforme a luz lhe dava" (26). The visual impression created by the "pomba's" position in relation to the crouching man varies, according to the light, between protection and conquest, neither pose casting the male figure in a powerful light. The epic self-images of men as gods and heroes are revealed to be ludicrously out of proportion to the fragile physical beings with whom Júlia forms a series of relationships.

The death of the male hero is most clearly elaborated when Júlia simultaneously juggles the amorous attentions of the old left and the old right. Mão Dianjo (the nickname for the more mundane Ernesto de Araújo) is a parody of the Marxist *resistente* generation. Deprived of the fulfilment of his revolutionary ideals and adapting to the new society, Mão Dianjo still sports a trendy ponytail. Nevertheless, his physical bulk and well being cause him to resemble one of life's first class passengers, "um banqueiro dos anos trinta, na First Class dum transatlântico cheio de salva-vidas" (226). His youthful memories of revolutionary Paris, "quando Paris era Paris" (266) reveal the sexism of his defunct Marxist pieties. Mão Dianjo conjures up the streets of Paris through the clichés of accordion music and Edith Piaf, admitting "ele que tinha sido um resistente, adorava a voz de mulheres decadentes" (266). He is outraged by Júlia's suggestion that they resolve the dilemma of her two partners with a

[11] See Jorge's interpretations of the "pomba" statue in Louro 1984.

"ménage à trois", and accuses her of being "uma burguesa enfastiada" (274). His own vision of the revolution takes the form of a sexual domination fantasy when he falls asleep and dreams he can hear the Russian tune Kalinka as he pursues Júlia transformed into "o meu sonho vermelho a fugir, a fugir diante do meu cavalo" (274). The contrasting figure of Saraiva, Júlia's wealthy Sesimbra-dwelling suitor, is a conservative middle-aged bachelor who revels in classic imperialist fiction such as *Minas de Salomão* and is dominated by his mother (302). When Júlia rejects him, he longs for another Colonial War so that he can go back to Angola. Mão Dianjo, similarly, gives up on the new Portugal and considers leaving his lifelong partner, Madalena, to go and live in Communist Hungary.

The space of the hero, which these two men leave conspicuously empty in Júlia's life is dramatically occupied by Artur Salema, the most physically imposing of the three sculptors. His dark, bearded appearance significantly echoes Anabela's as she too appears to have the dark shadow of a beard and moustache (320). Unaware of their similarity Anabela ironically nicknames *him* the "yeti", the mythical, sexually ambiguous Himalayan monster with breasts. Júlia's attempt at a settled relationship with Salema affords another postmodern take on the Ulysses topos, which is central to *Novas Cartas*. Júlia like Mariana does not depart and is therefore cast as the true adventurer and taker of risks. Moving through a series of different roles, images and countries of temporary residence. Salema is driven beyond himself by the romantic quest for new horizons in his art and his Marxist politics, although he still relies on Júlia for material support. When he first meets her he resembles the revolutionary Bakunin (41), only to discard this likeness when he departs for Switzerland leaving her behind (86-7). He subsequently returns from his travels "disfarçado de pedinte" (180) a direct allusion to Ulysses's return to Ithaca and in common with Ulysses, Artur is recognized by everyone except his "wife". Júlia, still angered by his departure does not want to accept him back but is finally won over.[12]

---

[12] Adriana Cavarero interestingly reads Penelope's non-identification of Ulysses as not a failure but a reluctance to recognize him on his return. Cavarero writes, "she doubts, she suspects,

When Júlia gets pregnant whilst Salema is unemployed, she fears she will be remembered by future generations as "seis cordas torcidas numa só" (229) the ropes of a ship's rigging reduced to a single umbilical cord and mooring Salema to a home of frustration and regret. The escape route of suicide, suggested by Salema's possession of a gun, is not available to Júlia, who has maternal responsibility for Jóia.[13] Rather, she opts for abortion as the only way to keep afloat the "frágil jangada de ervas" (228) on which they are sailing now that their ship has metaphorically been sunk. Her experience of the abortion is evoked through the inverted heroic quest of a nightmare journey through a "deserto que parecia eterno" (231). When she lies to Salema that she has lost the child, he "simulava uma incredulidade e uma solicitude alvoroçada como se de repente um navio lhe passasse diante dos olhos e estivesse embandeirado. As barbas davam-lhe o ar dum marinheiro" (233). Knowing that he must obey his compulsion to defy death by exploring the next horizon Júlia sends him away to Italy, "para nos salvarmos à vista da última margem" (234).

The postcard which Salema sends Júlia endeavours to validate the sacrificial costs (for her) of the journey of discovery he is making without her as he writes, "*valeu a pena, amor*. Também dizia que a Terra era redonda, os aviões velocíssimos e a esperança ilimitada" (239). Salema's heroic quest meets its ultimate satirical inversion, however, in the images at Fernando Rita's exhibition. It is suggested that one of Rita's exhibits has been named "Cavaleiro de Avallon", King Arthur, in memory of Artur Salema. It transpires that Salema has settled into married bourgeois domesticity, shaved and cut his hair resembling not the Knight of Avallon but Jack Nicholson at the end of *One Flew Over the Cuckoo's Nest* (283). He has never fulfilled himself as an artist and it is with his short, unglamorous and humble former work mate, Fernando Rita, that Júlia

she demands evidence. Perhaps, then, she does not want to recognize him. Or else, before the intrusion of the great event to which she will have to yield, she demonstrates that her symbolic space was not the expectation of Odysseus' return" (13-14).

[13] See Jorge's interview with Almeida Martins for autobiographical accounts of her own father as "um homem interessante, aventureiro, dinâmico" (6) who told tall tales of his extensive travels and kept a pistol under the mattress in their home in the Algarve.

eventually finds a companion, as well as deriving her own sense of creativity. Salema's final "imprisonment" in marriage prefigures the similar fate of his feminine surrogate, Anabela, who locks herself into a room for her own safety when confronted with Júlia's violent rebellion.

Júlia significantly turns the tables on Anabela and cuts off her influence in a dramatic reassertion of artistic autonomy. She had tried, throughout the novel, to make a living through the "traditionally" feminine art of sewing rag dolls. Indeed Júlia explicitly compares sculpture and doll making as she comments, "fazer escultura era alguma coisa bem mais séria do que criar bonecos" (32). The dolls are apparently sold via an intermediary, Ana de Lencastre. Although Júlia believes them to have been acquired by genuine customers, it transpires that Anabela herself has bought them all in order to support Júlia financially without telling her, in a grandiloquently patronizing act of charity and control. Júlia is horrified that Anabela has diverted her creative intentions for the dolls, their meticulously stitched individuality refusing the Platonic production line of a series of copies.

> Juro-lhe que fui fazendo essas bonecas imaginando que umas iriam enfeitar cadeiras, outras ficariam penduradas numa sala de entrada, outras por cima de camas, porque sabia que não se destinavam a crianças mas a adultos, mesmo quando compradas em nome de crianças. (319)

The sight of the functionally "aborted" rag dolls left to get damp and ruined arouses Júlia's anger as she prepares to confront Anabela comparing her feelings with those of an empathetic god looking down on suffering humanity in a reaffirmation of "a afeição, esta chamada sem destino próprio" (319).

Anabela's excessive belief in the truth of representation leads to her downfall. Where Anabela has always nicknamed Jóia "the Hulk" and the poisoning has indeed turned him green, it is actually Júlia who is about to emulate the hero of the 1970s American TV series, in which a mild-mannered scientist is transfigured by rage into a destructive green monster. Júlia's impending metamorphosis leaves a semiotic trail through the triple pun on the word "mona", signifying rag doll and female monkey, but also homonymous with

Leonardo da Vinci's Mona Lisa. The connection is unwittingly underlined by Anabela herself as she remarks to Júlia "estás sempre na mesma, sempre linda, giocondíssima, o que tens feito?" (315) but Jóia is not the Hulk and Júlia is not the Gioconda. The silent, enigmatic feminine as the transcendental absence of meaning in art connects the Mona Lisa with the stone sphinx of the "Pomba" referred to above, marking the site of Júlia's return in a newly embodied format. Her characteristic refusal to respond to Anabela with speech gives way to non-verbalized rage at Anabela's insensitivity about Jóia's suicide attempt. Consciously assuming the guise of a wolf, Júlia throws a knife at Anabela deliberately to miss and Anabela locks herself in a room and dials for help. Júlia links this act of violence to the first time she threw the knife, fending off the possessive abuses of Mão Dianjo in an "espelunca da Rua da Conceição" (320). Returning to the (Platonic) cave space, Júlia effectively overturns Anabela's representational order, teaching her that "a Terra se move de vários modos" (320). There is no single, dominant model for reproducing the spatial mechanics of the universe as the competing Ptolemaic and Copernican systems insist.

As Jorge herself points out, Anabela "faz mimetismo do homem; Júlia é talvez a personagem por onde a mudança passa realmente" (Louro 1984, 2). Júlia's attempt to mimic Anabela produces a false copy or as Antónia de Sousa puts it, "quando esta [Júlia] quer macaquear o que a outra faz não vai conseguir. A Júlia Grey (sic) acaba por ser um travesti" (1985, 6). It is precisely this failure to copy Anabela which frees Júlia not only from Anabela as "uma pessoa exemplar que me torturava a vida" (245) but also from the tyranny of the hierarchical model. By behaving as a travesty or simulacrum she de-authorizes the original and proudly rediscovers, "as artes de dissumular" (312) learned from childhood with tales such as Little Red Riding Hood. Through her act of defence, Júlia empathetically reincorporates herself into the human race defined simply as a group of somatic beings who share the capacity to suffer. Even Mão Dianjo, with his posturing arrogance and physical bulk, was also born of woman, as Júlia implies when she listens to his speeches and fixes her eyes on "a barriga de Mão Dianjo redonda, com um umbigo muito fundo ao centro" (301). Her throwing of the knife is, ultimately, the cutting of one cord and the tying of another (like Penelope?) a gesture of identification with all that is human in a group of unsymbolized bodies who need to make a fundamental assertion of their capacity for survival. Walking through the streets Júlia observes the flow of people disembarking from the ferry:

> Gente baixa, gente gorda, gente negra, gente de poderosas varizes como rios de sangue, gente anã, gente coxa, gente torta carregada de sacos de plástico. Como seirões de trigo e estrume que devessem ser transportados sobre azémolas. Gente igual a mim, gente minha irmã. Gente ainda por meter medo a alguém pelo menos uma vez na vida. Gente mutiplamente em silêncio. (321)

Leaving Anabela locked in the building, Júlia thinks "meto medo logo existo, logo existo, logo existo, Jóia existe, o Fernando existe" (321) displacing the Cartesian "cogito" from the rational sphere to the physical and material realm of non-rational embodiment as the resurgence of "subjectivity". With this gesture she posits the co-existence of the other(s), not their dualistic elimination. As Jorge herself has suggestively remarked of this novel, "de resto, nesta história, pus muito pouco de cérebro" (Louro 1984, 2). Júlia returns the knife to V. from whom she had borrowed it, linking her writing and the weapon as tools of physical survival.

Cartesian "being" has been displaced supplanted by "becoming", echoing the Deleuzian conceptualization of writing as an act of creativity which requires one to "become minor" and "marginal" in a way that women in particular already potentially are. For Deleuze "la minorité, c'est le devenir de tout le monde, son devenir potentiel pour autant qu'il dévie du modèle" (1978, 154). Women, already possessing "minor" status in relation to "major" power, regardless of their actual numbers, have a particular position within this process:

> Les femmes, quelque soit leur nombre, sont une minorité définissable comme état ou sous-ensemble: mais elles ne créent qu'en rendant possible un devenir, dont elles n'ont pas la propriété, dans lequel elles ont elles-memes à entrer, un devenir-femme qui concerne l'homme tout entier, les non-femmes y compris. (1978, 155)

The dynamic, mobile "becoming-woman" or "becoming-minority" thus goes beyond the dualistic oppositions of majority and minority, making a creative virtue of displacement and transition, also more popularly theorized by Deleuze and Guattari as "becoming nomad" or "nomadology".[14] As Rosi Braidotti has pointed out in her discussion of Deleuze and Guattari, this becoming woman or minor has no necessary relation to the lived experience of women, real minorities or their acquisition of agency. As she asks, "I wonder whether the theory of positive and multiple desire does not finally result in women's disappearance from the scene of history, their fading-out as agents of history" (1991, 119). Jorge counters the all too easy Deleuzian elision of women's lived asymmetries of power into undifferentiated affect by showing maternity, in particular, as historically subject to discipline and containment. This is exemplified in the novel's two illegal abortions, precipitated by the essentially romantic construction of the female body as the nomad's infinite space, the "bad nomadism" which Salema and Anabela pursue and which Júlia displaces.

The final separation of Júlia from Anabela is described as the long slow farewell of an embarkation. Júlia repeats at intervals "adeus, Anabela" and "aceno-te de muito longe" (321) as if a ship were slowly leaving the quay. Echoing the opening chapter in the closing one, Júlia sees a ship arriving and departing, "como um barco descarregava gente àquele hora" (321) but here it is an internal domestic ferry, not an ocean-going liner. Anabela, who had begun by dominating the city, is finally contained in a room and paralyzed by her fear. It is Júlia who finally "departs" but the departure is not the fanatical desire-driven quest to discover, subjugate and conquer space. On that level, Júlia also allegorically configures the "becoming minor" of a semiperipheric Portugal, the national "travessia" of the end of an empire.

The poetic voice which Júlia acquires results from a private moment of "renaissance", a resurgence of somatically registered sensation, of becoming rather than being, whilst she is waiting for news of Jóia from his callous,

[14] See Ferreira 1999, 111n and Owen 1999a, 90-93 on Deleuze and Guattari's theories of "minor" literature as relevant to Jorge.

scientifically-obsessed doctor. She reacts against the doctor's world view in which "o raciocínio e o sentimento duma pessoa ficam simples como um tubérculo de batata, pele de cortiça, polpa branca" (296). Suddenly conscious of the "other city", the original "cidade silvestre" of the title as a nostalgic fantasy, a buried memory within, she becomes certain that "a outra margem da rua principal era uma zona silvestre de que este lado era apenas uma lembrança selvagem" (297). This inspires her to an endless flow of words on the pages of her usually regimented diary. As Jorge has indicated in interview, the meaning of "notícia" is to be understood here not as news of everyday events but as primal memory "lembrança de um tempo primordial que a vida nesta terra recorda" (Louro 1984, 3).

Júlia gives voice to "conhecer", the intimate, emotional act of "knowing" as a kind of understanding which overturns Anabela's empiricist "saber", recalling the two categories into which Anabela had divided the world, inspired by the empires of "Alexandre Magno e Napoleão" (54). Those who belong to the "conhecer" category are people who "apenas vislumbrava dados fugidios como uma árvore a andar, um pingo de chuva a cair, sem saber transformar o que vislumbrava na matéria orgânica do proveito" (200). Jóia is also saved from retreating into "saber" as the excessive pursuit of rational humanist epistemologies. His room is full of scientific implements and his increasingly disturbed state of mind is manifested through a mania for drawing straight, parallel lines as if, in the manner of a latter-day navigator, he wished to map and conquer new space. Preoccupied by Jóia's obsession with "ciências abstractas que aplicava a astronomia" (272) Júlia tries to reintroduce the biosciences into his thinking by reminding him that "a Zoologia e a Botânica eram partes da Matemática" (279). Jóia's excessively disciplinary world view and his ultimately literal withdrawal from the world of the living are finally overcome by his creative attachment to Fernando Rita, who takes over David Grei's sculpture studio.

Júlia's own artistic maturation reaches completion when she leaves Sr. Assumpção's employment, having wearied of the dead western metaphysics sedimented on his shelves as she amusingly indicates with her ecological fantasy of the bookshop as simply a slaughterhouse of trees (280-1). Júlia writes in conclusion that, "o papel é um tecido doce, humano e envolvente como uma pele [...] como se a partir dessa frágil matéria, sentisse e pudesse dar notícia da outra realidade" (322). The paper as "pele" connotes both parchment and skin, emphasizing Júlia's sense of writing as a new form of embodiment. As her ethical mode of fantasy explores a world turned inwards, she embarks on a new "epic" journey through a universe of affect unbound by any necessary correspondence to the illusory contingencies of reproducing objective truth. As she point out, "só às vezes a luz coincide com a sombra, mas tão breves são estes momentos e tão raras vezes sucedem na vida, que melhor é esperar por um significado que amadureça dentro. Ainda que inventado. Amadureceu"(308). The internal disparities rather than coincidences which emerge between her diaries and her "papéis" have produced a play of images as space in-between, the chiaroscuro of the city, expressing a time of "penumbra", an entr'acte in which "o mundo abre, fecha sua cortina, a vida transfigura-se" (322).

Fernando Rita's sculptures of fruit lead to the productive recycling of old mythologies as he introduces Júlia to a new artistic vision which has dispensed with the specular representation of the body as sexed. Near the end of the novel, Rita fashions a series of horse sculptures curiously entitled "Éguas". Although they are labelled mares, Júlia cannot decide what sex they really are as "representavam seres equídeos a que eu não saberia atribuir sexo, nem me importava, era lá com ele" (282). She subsequently discovers that Rita was inspired by an ancient story about the mares of Lisbon who produce the heroes of the future, impregnated by the wind blowing through their manes and tales. This shared vision not of heroes reborn but of artistic fantasy itself undergoing a regeneration inspires Júlia's belief in "um dia longínquo, se alguma vez houver tempo para um pensamento sereno como o que cria os mitos e a magia" (307).

In conclusion Júlia transforms a mundane, anti-heroic scene into the magical image of a new beginning as she describes Rita, Jóia and the other sculptors cooperatively spitting and rubbing to clean the layers of red dust off the windscreen of Rita's Zephyr.[15] When Rita drives away he is endearingly described in mock-heroic mode, bump-starting his old car. He is also referred to as Júlia's "ex-visita", the implication being that he will henceforth no longer relate to her in a casual manner. Looking back at Júlia as he turns the corner, Rita effects a hesitant departure that is also a backward glance at the past. The novel thus ends with "um bom dia para recomeçar" (322) and the "other city" casts a cinematographic aura over the scene as "uma campânula duma outra fosforescência desceu sobre a rua inteira" (322).

It could be argued of Jorge, as it has been of Deleuze and Guattari, that the aesthetic impulse of nomadology relies on essentially European modernist figurations of the margin, the exile and infinite space, even as it displaces the humanist power structures behind the colonialist project (Kaplan, C. 85-100). However, the utopia which *Notícia* envisions if any is a chastened self-reflexive fantasy of the elsewhere, which retains a sense of its responsibilities to the material here and now. As an ambiguously mediated piece of personal testimony turned postmodern art, *Notícia* re-orientates the romance of infinite displacement and the power of fantasy into creatively rethinking narrative fiction itself in terms which allow for philosophy as well as politics. Lídia Jorge has remarked on the intellectual hiatus of the mid-1980s "terminadas as ideologias, removem-se as ideias. Vivemos um tempo em que uma coisa nova começou, somos intérpretes e ainda não lhe demos nome. Não é importante experimentar o caos?" (Almeida Martins 6).

Jorge's narrative project in *Notícia* retains a necessarily political dimension nonetheless in its rejection of the specific technologies of gender materially and imaginatively sustaining the latter-day expansionist impulses exemplified by Salema and Anabela. The dream of the other city, the "campânula duma outra fosforescência" (322), the "noumos" within the "polis", connects Júlia and Rita in a shared artistic vision, no longer sustained by the kind of sexual

---

[15] See Pazos Alonso 1999b, 41 for interesting symbolic readings of the Zephyr as the God of the west wind connecting with the impregnation of the mares, and also for a compelling argument that Fernando Rita himself is presented as an angelic, androgynous figure.

hierarchy or its representation, which licensed territorial appropriation of the exotic other as colonialist fantasy. In this respect, *Notícia* also makes a fictionalized intervention in the quest for new beginnings in language, literature and culture which marked the 1984 commemorative reflections on the tenth anniversary of the revolution. As the reign of political monologue and monologics is overtaken by the call for new forms of dialogue (Pintasilgo 1986, 68), Jorge paradigmatically rejects women's historical role as "ventríloquas dos homens" (Almeida Martins 10). Pushing the cutting edge of her creative expression towards a fable for the 1980s, Jorge makes the "mais algum proveito" (17) to which V. referred at the outset, the dividend of a moral over an economic benefit to be derived from a speaking with, not a speaking for.

CONCLUSION

Writing the Unfinished Revolution

O chão da revolução não é a morte da diferença, nem o bom
riso está à flor da mão. O chão da revolução é a morte do valor
da diferença, de todas as diferenças. (*Novas Cartas* 300)

To conclude by tracing thematic and poetic connections between such diverse
women writers as those studied in this volume is a project which, perhaps
inevitably, risks homogenizing and essentializing the very right to differences
between women which the generation of the revolution had fought to secure.
However, certain points of contact are discernible nonetheless in so far as their
writings responded to the various ways in which the right to multiple difference
remained compromised and controversial in the world of the post-revolution.
Virgínia Ferreira has pointed to the slow growth of individualistic lifestyles and
Portugal's process of "industrialization without modernization" (163) as powerful
socio-cultural factors which militated against the enactment of women's rights.
Lídia Jorge has also interestingly remarked in this respect that "the family still
seems as if a given by nature rather than culture" (d'Orey 168). It is this
persistence of the family paradigm, as the preferred locus for registering progress,
stasis and dissidence in women's writing which serves as point of entry for my
concluding remarks.

The patriarchal family is dramatically "posta em causa" by the Three
Marias' dismantling of genealogy, but the heterosexual contract as the base of
society is left open to renegotiation by the women writers of the post-revolution.

In *Paisagem*, Hortense and Clara are left paralyzed by the loss of Horácio and Pedro. The Marxist model of the resistant "povo" with which the novel concludes can only countenance the inclusion of women according to heterosexual reproductive relations such as those implied by Hortense's new lover and Clara's child. In *Montedemo* the white, western humanist myth of paternity is pushed to an extreme, through the positing of its absolute loss. No father can be found or imagined for the illegitimate mulatto child. Society responds violently to the abject maternal body and to the absence of the (white) father from this alternative "Holy Family". *Mandei-lhe uma Boca* and *Sara* trace the return to paternal authority, albeit secular and intellectual, through the Freudian, psychoanalyst father whom Sara had previously condemned for his hypocritical affairs. In *Sara* she values and accepts her father's judgement, having transferred much of her resentment to her similarly adulterous mother. The heterosexual family norm thus remains the key structuring element of the novel and the metafictional, double conclusion is triggered by Diogo's possible paternity of a child by another woman. Sara is left to create her fictional identity through the image of her grandmother's ring which reaffirms her sense of belonging to the kind of genealogical lineage which *Novas Cartas* had sought to delegitimize. Where the first three writers of the post-revolution deal effectively with the western humanist mythologies behind Estado Novo paternalism, Jorge goes a step further by killing off the Marxist "fathers of the revolution" metaphorically in the case of Mão Dianjo, and literally in the case of David Grei. The novel exposes, nonetheless, the social difficulties of a widowed mother raising a fatherless son in a context where the ideological radicalism of the revolution has not substantially revised the family script. The anti-representational, deterritorialized artistic vision which connects Fernando Rita, Júlia and Jóia at the end of *Notícia* gestures towards the invention of a contingent "family" in a non-Oedipalized social space. However, the "monsterization" of Anabela precisely for her lack of maternal feeling remains a disquieting element in the novel not wholly resolved.

A recurrent trope through all of the texts is the absence of the father as a result of colonial war, death, migration, professional commitment or zest for adventure. Maria-Antionetta Macciocchi's analysis of family mythology under Mussolini's fascist regime, has suggested that the discursive suppression of "real" fathers in favour of the symbolic One, went hand in hand with the implantation of fascist mythologies of hyper-paternalism. She writes, "au long du discours, les variations mussoliniennes sur les fils sont telles que les fils semblent ne pouvoir parler que de pères putatifs: ils sont 'fils de martyrs', de 'mutilés', fils de 'jeunes couples paysans' [...] *Finalement, ils n'ont jamais de pères*" (36). In contrast to Il Duce's famously hyperbolic machismo Salazarist paternalism was, of course, ideologically robed in an ambiguous image of celibate priesthood, but it operated symbolically nonetheless as a powerful pseudo-transcendental locus of authority. Read in this light, the tentative move to reinscribe the "real" father into the social discourses of the new order, marks the call for a new non-authoritarian family, less vulnerable to the resurgence of fascist hyper-paternalisms, a move further reinforced through the death of transcendental paternity in anti-humanist poetics.

Ana Paula Ferreira's readings of post-revolutionary women writers, including Gersão, Gonçalves and Jorge, argue that their female characters are, "culturally equipped by their very tangential position in the symbolic order to question the meanings, the political function and value of its language, thereby opening breaches in that order" (1997 237). Since women's ambivalent relationship to symbolic language questions the founding contracts of society, their formation as subjects in non-oppositional dialogic relation to the "other" (of race, gender, social class, childhood or old age) suggests possible new forms of community. Ferreira's Kristevan-inspired reading of the feminine as dissidence in poetic language (1986, 292-300) concludes that the "almost Orphic renaming of the world from a woman's point of view" (237) acts as a semiotic interruption or temporary act of suspension disturbing the dominant symbolic of the unitary masculine call to revolution. By the same token, she argues they allow for a self-reflexive critique of the dominant, historical narratives of revolution as well as their own. Part of this auto-reflection in the present study has taken the form of exploiting the gaps and disjunctures which emerge between the freedom of the word and the relative unfreedom of the body in the immediate post-revolutionary context. Woman's body remained patriarchally overwritten and devoid of autonomous desire within left-wing discourses of a sexually neutral "povo". There is an eerie ring to the words of the anonymous woman interviewee from the MDM whose anti-abortionist views were cited in *Big Flame* in 1975. "We don't think it's a priority. We have to be careful – after all, Portugal will need more people to industrialise successfully" (24).

All of the works I discuss show women attempting to go beyond the fate which the Three Marias so eloquently named when they wrote, "a mulher só é dado o parir e o parado" (83). In *Novas Cartas* and the novels which followed it, women are reborn to themselves and their own desire through the inscription of the somatic into poetic language, as they assume power over the representational codes delineating their physical limits as embodied subjects in space. Their insistence on the sexually differentiated body opens the way to new considerations of the body *per se* in post-revolutionary poetics. Where subjectivity is never fixed in one delimited bodily space, they engage in various forms of what one might term "hetero-corporeality" a process of speaking as embodied self in and through the body of the other, as the Three Marias paradigmatically do. This is evident in the inexpressible empathy between Hortense and Clara in *Paisagem*. In *Montedemo* new forms of knowing, with which the narrator is complicit, are vested in the transgressive, irrational bodies of women, animals and children. In *Sara*, the heroine realizes that she can never empathize with Guilherme because he is alien to her philosophical search for "leis sábias, sem ameaça, com apreço e lugar para todas as espécies à superfície do mundo" (164). Júlia Grei's personal "cogito" in *Notícia* is precisely only expressible through her sense of connection to "gente igual a mim, gente minha irmã. Gente ainda por meter medo a alguém pelo menos uma vez na vida. Gente multiplamente em silêncio" (321). A necessary condition of this discourse, however, is the assertion of women's right to voice the delimitations of their corporeal space, most saliently expressed in the late 1970s and early 1980s through the right to control reproduction and to obtain abortion.

Abortion remained illegal, even in the limited terms of the 1984 act, at the time when all the novels except *Sara* (1986) were written. *Montedemo* is the only text studied here which does not refer directly to women's experiences of illegal abortion. Even there, Correia does effectively undermine the anti-abortion case by exposing the hypocrisies and repressions inherent in a maternalist Catholic rhetoric which does not scruple to destroy a child when it is an illegitimate mulatto. In *Novas Cartas*, Mariana implicitly aborts the child she accidentally conceives with the cavalier in the convent and the Marias bear witness to the deaths of working class women, such as the office cleaner who dies of septicaemia following a back street abortion. In *Paisagem*, Clara tries to escape single motherhood under Salazarism by attempting suicide while pregnant, the only solution she can see in a world with no support for widowed mothers. Gonçalves's *Sara* paints a picture of the isolated, frightening experience of clandestine abortion for a young middle-class woman in the 1980s, who becomes aware that doctors are undermining the law with their own "micro-revoltas" (103) and uses a women's underground information network to exchange addresses and contacts. *Notícia* approaches the problem from the angle of social class as both Anabela and Júlia are economically forced into having terminations and fall into the hands of an unscrupulous extortionist. Júlia's abortion in particular is contrasted with Artur Salema's ability to avoid such problems by taking the traditionally masculine option to go and work abroad. Julia Kristeva has suggested, "real female innovation [...] will only come about when maternity, female creativity and the link between them are better understood" (1986a, 298) but the necessary political obverse of this must be the realization that abortion and women's relationship to violence and death also inform that innovative creativity.

As I argued in my first chapter, *Novas Cartas* sought to delegitimize the sacrifice of women's bodies and desires as the hidden cost of the heroic utopian ideal, the quest for the transcendental phallic absolute in imperialism, fascism, or Marxist revolution. Lídia Jorge has interestingly written of the new literature which emerged in the 1980s that it was "something like a transfiguration... of the reality; the reality itself is present with all its fundamentals but the poetic transfiguration surfaces very strongly, violently; it is a violent writing" (Kaufman and Klobucka 19). The new aesthetics of embodiment which women writers developed, effectively sought to account for the realities of both maternity and abortion by questioning the sacrificial exclusion of the body of woman as the condition of representational narrative. This was already signalled, in a sense, in *Novas Cartas* where the Three Marias discussed the right to define and defend the limits of their own bodies in terms of the limits of the poetic project in which they were engaged:

> Não sei quem excluímos, quem matamos. [...] Fizemos a ara, a taça, o vinho, olhamo-nos de soslaio e perguntamos 'quem imolamos, quem vencemos, quem usamos?'. Mas já matámos, já excluímos; sugámos-lhe o sangue, o jogo e as armas [...] Foi dita a gravidade desta empresa, luta de vida, o que em nosso tempo e nosso sítio não é tido por legítimo, nem por defesa. (48)

As the two narratives of unfinished revolution, the Marxist and the sexual one, fall increasingly out of step, differently gendered memories emerge into the spaces created by women's position simultaneously inside and outside the "common" memories of the past. The inside and outside of gender in de Lauretis's concept of the "space-off", are here transposed into the collective ideologies of the "nation" and "people". This narrative double-vision as the symptom of alternative memory is most clearly discernible through the changing use of subject pronoun positions and narrative focalizations across the various works. *Novas Cartas* is the polyphonic drama *par excellence* and the Marias' habitual bracketing of alternative subject pronouns alongside those which govern the verb, allows no one subject to wield a monologic syntactical authority over the recording of experience. In *Paisagem*, the initial proliferation of (suicidal) infinitives gives way to the merging of subject pronoun positions, foreshadowing the inclusion of Clara and Hortense in the community of the "povo" as provisional, discursive unity. In *Montedemo* the polyphonic focus is replaced by a third person narrator, who recreates in microcosm the process by which oral memory is expressed as collective narrative. Milena's violent abjection from the community, as a condition of its expression as such, exposes the ways in which deep-rooted cultural constructions of femininity militate against their equal integration in the imagined totality of the peasant mass. In *Sara* and *Notícia* the third person narrator functions as a device to introduce a confessional first person which works productively between the genres of diary, testimonial and *Bildungsroman* turned *Künstlerroman*. At this decisive juncture, women's voices are no longer contingent on the legitimizing discourses of the revolution, the collective, the "povo" or the end of empire. Rather they refocalize these themes retrospectively and independently in the ongoing narrative of women's coming to writing in self-consciously individual performance of their newly acquired scriptural roles.

As bourgeois evolution replaced Socialist revolution as the guiding narrative of progress, individualism supplanted the old collective, instrumentalist priorities and the pursuit of highly personalized literary aesthetics signalled a "coming of age" for women's writing in particular. Having decisively reclaimed the body as a site of literary and linguistic articulation, women writers endeavoured as far as possible to normalize their participation in the new literary initiatives, which pushed beyond the "tempo suspenso" of transition. As the women writers studied in this volume effectively recognize, the unwriting of a certain History was a condition of their writing at all, the process which Graça Abranches has described as an "un-learning in order to speak" (1998b). Re-inscribing their past experiences in non-monumental forms of poetics enabled them to be part of a rapidly changing literary future that could accommodate the "revoluções minúsculas" (Pintasilgo 1986, 66) of their many and potential selves. As the assertion of 1970s feminism began to seem outmoded and unnecessary, the predominant concept of literary aesthetics emphasized formal neutrality and integration into a single canon. The image of aesthetic androgyny which Lídia Jorge evoked in her admiration of Woolf's *Orlando* serves effectively to characterize the way in which many women writers of the 1980s accurately perceived their writing as part of the move to normalize and consolidate women's presence within mainstream literary production. That they do so, well into the

1980s, with one eye on the clock of history, suggests their continued awareness nonetheless of the pervasive technologies of gender writing the past within the present. Where their bold reinventions of literary language remain in dialogue with society as discursive community, they demonstrate that the angel of literature may well be androgynous, but the ghosts of history have a sex.

BIBLIOGRAPHY

1. Primary Texts

Barreno, Maria Isabel, Maria Teresa Horta and Maria Velho da Costa. 1998. *Novas Cartas Portuguesas*. Lisboa: Dom Quixote.

Correia, Hélia. 1987. *Montedemo*. Lisboa: Relógio d'Água.

Gersão, Teolinda. 1985. *Paisagem com Mulher e Mar ao Fundo*. Lisboa: O Jornal.

Gonçalves, Olga. 1983. *Mandei-lhe uma Boca*. Lisboa: Livraria Bertrand.

Gonçalves, Olga. 1986b. *Sara*. Lisboa: Caminho.

Jorge, Lídia. 1984. *Notícia da Cidade Silvestre*. Lisboa: Europa-América.

2. Secondary Texts

II Congresso dos Escritores Portugueses. n.d. *Discursos, Comunicações, Debates, Moções, Saudações*. Lisboa: Associação Portuguesa de Escritores e Publicações Dom Quixote.

Abel, Elizabeth, Marianne Hirsch and Elizabeth Langland, eds. 1983. *The Voyage in: Fictions of Female Development*. Hanover: University Press of New England.

Abranches, Graça. 1998a. "'On what terms shall we join the procession of educated men?' Teaching Feminist Studies at the University of Coimbra." Centro de Estudos Sociais 125. Coimbra: Oficina do CES.

——. 1998b. "Unlearning in order to speak: politics, writings and poetics of Portuguese women of the twentieth century." Unpublished paper delivered to the Spanish and Portuguese Studies Department seminar, University of Manchester, 23 April.

Acheson, Dean. 1987. *Present at the Creation. My Years in the State Department.* New York and London: W. W. Norton.

Alexandre, Valentim. 1998. "The Colonial Empire." Pinto, *Modern Portugal* 41-59.

Baptista, Luís A. Vicente. 1986. "Valores e imagens da família em Portugal nos anos 30 – o quadro normativo." *A Mulher na Sociedade Portuguesa. Visão Histórica e Perspectivas Actuais. Colóquio 20 –22 de Março de 1985. Actas* Vol. 1. Coimbra: Instituto de História Económica e Social, Universidade de Coimbra. 2 vols. 191-219.

Barbosa, Madalena. 1981. "Women in Portugal." *Women's Studies International Quarterly* 4.4: 477-480.

Belo, Maria, Ana Paula Alão and Iolanda Neves Cabral. 1987. "O Estado Novo e as Mulheres." *O Estado Novo. Das Origens ao Fim da Autarcia. 1926-1959.* Lisboa: Fragmentos. 263-79.

Besse, Maria Graciete. 2000. *Os limites da alteridade na ficção de Olga Gonçalves.* Porto: Campo das Letras.

Bhabha, Homi K. 1985. "Signs Taken for Wonders: Questions of Ambivalence and Authority under a Tree outside Delhi, May 1817." Ed. Francis Barker et al. *Europe and its Others.* Colchester: University of Essex. 80-106.

——. 1990. "DissemiNation: time, narrative, and the margins of the modern nation." *Nation and Narration.* London and New York: Routledge. 291-322.

Big Flame. n.d. *Portugal. A Blaze of Freedom.* Birmingham: Big Flame Publications.

Birmingham, David. 1993. *A Concise History of Portugal.* Cambridge: Cambridge University Press.

Braidotti, Rosi. 1991. *Patterns of Dissonance. A Study of Women in Contemporary Philosophy.* Trans. Elizabeth Guild. Cambridge: Polity Press.

——. 1994. *Nomadic Subjects. Embodiment and Sexual Difference in Contemporary Feminist Theory.* New York: Columbia University Press.

Brum, Eduardo J. and José F. Tavares. 1987. Interview with Hélia Correia. "'Não Gosto do Vampirismo do Público'." *Signo. Jornal de Letras e Artes* Fevereiro: 6-7.

Bulger, Laura. 1988. "A propósito de Sara." *Letras e Letras* 1 de Outubro: 11.

Calvino, Italo. 1974. *Invisible Cities*. Trans. William Weaver. London: Secker and Warburg.

Camões, Luís de. 1980. *Os Lusíadas*. Ed. Emanuel Paulo Ramos. Porto: Porto Editora.

Cavarero, Adriana. 1995. *In Spite of Plato. A Feminist Rewriting of Ancient Philosophy*. Trans. Serena Anderlini-D'Onofrio and Áine O'Healey. Cambridge: Polity Press.

Chiote, Eduarda. 1988. "Olga Gonçalves: A literatura que eu produzo será sempre a do 'eu estava là!'." *Letras e Letras* 1 de Outubro: 12.

Comissão para a Igualdade e para os Direitos das Mulheres. 1995. *Portugal Situação das Mulheres*. Lisboa.

Correia, Hélia. 1996. "O Surpeendente Pequeno Mundo - A Escrita Feminina." Owen, *Gender, Ethnicity and Class* 49-62.

D'Arthuys, Béatrice. 1976. *As Mulheres Portuguesas e o 25 de Abril*. Porto: Afrontamento.

De Lauretis, Teresa. 1988. "Feminist Studies/Critical Studies: Issues, Terms, and Contexts." *Feminist Studies/Critical Studies*. Ed. Teresa de Lauretis. Basingstoke: Macmillan. 1-19.

——. 1989. *Technologies of Gender. Essays on Theory, Film, and Fiction*. Basingstoke: Macmillan.

Deleuze, Gilles. 1978. "Philosophie et Minorité." *Critique. Revue générale des publications françaises et étrangères* Février: 154-5.

——. 1983. "Plato and the Simulacrum." Trans. Rosalind Krauss. *October* 27: 45-56.

Dionísio, Eduarda. 1993. *Títulos, Acções, Obrigações. (Sobre a Cultura em Portugal, 1974-1994)*. Lisboa: Edições Salamandra.

D'Orey, Stephanie. 1999. Interview with Lídia Jorge. Trans. Stephanie D'Orey with the assistance of John Brooksmith. *Lídia Jorge. in other words/por outras palavras*. Ed. Cláudia Pazos Alonso. Special issue of *Portuguese Literary and Cultural Studies* 2: 167-74.

Duarte, Luiz Fagundes. 1986. Review. "'Sara'. Aventuras na aldeia portuguesa." *Jornal de Letras* 17 de Novembro: 29.

——. 1988. "Para que servem os romancistas." *Letras e Letras* 1 de Outubro: 8.

Engelmayer, Elfriede und Renate Hess, eds. 1993. *Die Schwestern der Mariana Alcoforado. Portuguiesische Schriftstellerinnen der Gegenwart.* Berlin: Edition Tranvía. Verlag Walter Frey.

Ferreira, Ana Paula. 1989. "Para uma história-mulher: *Ora esguardae*, de Olga Gonçalves." *Luso-Brazilian Review* 26.2: 11-23.

——. 1993. "Discursos femininos, teoria crítica feminista: para uma resposta que não é." *Discursos Femininos.* Special issue of *Discursos. Estudos de Língua e Cultura Portuguesa* 5: 13-27.

——. 1996. "Home Bound: The Construct of Femininity in the Estado Novo." *Portuguese Studies* 12: 133-144.

——. 1997. "Reengendering History: Women's Fictions of the Portuguese Revolution." Kaufman and Klobucka, *After the Revolution* 219-42.

——. 1999. "Donning the 'Gift' of Representation: Lídia Jorge's *A Instrumentalina.*" *Lídia Jorge. in other words/por outras palavras.* Ed. Cláudia Pazos Alonso. Special issue of *Portuguese Literary and Cultural Studies* 2: 99-112.

Ferreira, Virgínia. 1998. "Engendering Portugal: Social Change, State Politics and Women's Social Mobilization." Pinto, *Modern Portugal* 162-188.

França, Elisabete. 1987. "Hélia Correia e a 'geração de 68', hoje." *Diário de Notícias* 1 Novembro: 4-5.

Freitas, Gina de. 1975. *A Força Ignorada das Companheiras. Diálogos.* Lisboa: Planalto.

Freud, Sigmund. 1991 *On Metapsychology: The Theory of Psychoanalysis.* Trans. James Strachey. Ed. Angela Richards. Vol. 11 of *The Penguin Freud Library.* 15 vols. London: Penguin.

Gallagher, Tom. 1983. *Portugal. A twentieth-century interpretation.* Manchester: Manchester University Press.

Gallop, Jane. 1985. *Reading Lacan.* Ithaca and London: Cornell University Press.

Gillespie, Faith. 1974. "The Women's Liberation Context." *Index on Censorship* 2: 22-6.

Gonçalves, Olga. 1986a. Interview with Olga Gonçalves. "Olga Gonçalves fala-
nos do seu romance 'Sara'." *O diário* 16 Novembro: 3-5.

——. 1987. "Olga, Sara e outras mais." *Mulheres* Janeiro: 24-6.

Goulart, Sandra Regina Almeida. 1994. "Writing from the Place of the Other:
The Poetic Discourse of Transgression in the Works of Virginia Woolf,
Clarice Lispector and Teolinda Gersão." Unpublished Dissertation.
University of North Carolina.

Guimarães, Maria João. 1998. "Novas cartas de ontem, velhas estórias de hoje."
Público 25 Novembro: 4-5.

Harsgor, Michael. 1976. *Portugal in Revolution*. Beverly Hills. Sage.

Hasebrink, Gisa. 1993. "Aufbrüche von Frauen und Künstlern in den fiktionalen
Welten von Teolinda Gersão." Engelmayer und Hess 103-118.

Horta, Maria Teresa. 1982a. Review of *Paisagem com Mulher e Mar ao Fundo*,
by Teolinda Gersão. *Mulheres* Dezembro: 76.

——. 1982b. "Três Marias... Dez Anos Depois." *Mulheres* Outubro: 4-6.

——. 1983. Review of *Montedemo*, by Hélia Correia. *Mulheres* Dezembro: 77.

——. 1984. Review of *Notícia da Cidade Silvestre*, by Lídia Jorge. "'Notícia da
Cidade Silvestre.' Novo romance de Lídia Jorge." *Mulheres* Dezembro:
11.

——. 1986. "*Novas Cartas*... Tantos Anos Depois." *Mulheres* Novembro: 33.

Hutcheon, Linda. 1988. *A Poetics of Postmodernism. History, Theory, Fiction*.
New York and London: Routledge.

Irigaray, Luce. 1985a. *Speculum of the Other Woman*. Trans. Gillian C. Gill.
Ithaca: Cornell University Press.

——. 1985b. *This Sex Which is Not One*. Trans. Catherine Porter with Carolyn
Burke. Ithaca: Cornell University Press.

Jorge, Lídia. 1986. "Escrita e Emancipação." *Revista Crítica de Ciências Sociais*
Fevereiro: 57-62.

——. 1989. "Orlando." *Jornal de Letras* 11-17 de Julho: 32.

——. 1993. "O soldado Herak." *Jornal de Letras* 23-29 de Março: 32.

Justo, Cipriano. 1984. Review. "'Montedemo' novela de Hélia Correia." *O diário*
4 Março: 12.

Kaplan, Caren. 1996. *Questions of Travel. Postmodern Discourses of Displacement*. Durham and London: Duke University Press.

Kaplan, Gisela. 1992. *Contemporary Western European Feminism*. North Sydney: Allen and Unwin; London: UCL Press.

Kauffman, Linda S. 1986. *Discourses of Desire. Gender, Genre and Epistolary Fictions*. Ithaca and London: Cornell University Press.

Kaufman, Helena and Anna Klobucka, eds. 1997a. *After the Revolution. Twenty Years of Portuguese Literature, 1974-1994*. Lewisburg: Bucknell University Press.

——. 1997b. "Politics and Culture in Postrevolutionary Portugal." Kaufman and Klobucka, *After the Revolution* 13-30.

Klobucka, Anna. 1993. "De autores e autoras." *Discursos Femininos*. Special issue of *Discursos. Estudos de Língua e Cultura Portuguesa* 5: 49-65.

——. 2000. *The Portuguese Nun: The Formation of a National Myth*. Lewisburg: Bucknell University Press.

Kong-Dumas, Catherine. 1983. Review of *Paisagem com Mulher e Mar ao Fundo*, by Teolinda Gersão. *Colóquio/Letras* Maio: 78-80.

Kristeva, Julia. 1982. *Powers of Horror. An Essay on Abjection*. Trans. Léon S. Roudiez. European Perspectives. New York: Columbia University Press.

——. 1986a. "A New Type of Intellectual: The Dissident." Trans. Seán Hand. Moi 292-300.

——. 1986b. "Stabat Mater." Trans. Léon S. Roudiez. Moi 160-86.

——. 1986c. "Women's Time." Trans. Alice Jardine and Harry Blake. Moi 187-213.

Labovitz, Esther Kleinbord. 1986. *The Myth of the Heroine. The Female Bildungsroman in the Twentieth Century*. Series XIX. General Literature 4. New York: Peter Lang.

Lacan, Jacques. 1977. *Écrits. A Selection*. Trans. Alan Sheridan. London: Routledge.

Letria, José Jorge. 1983. Interview with Hélia Correia. "Estamos a deixar de ser uma província da Europa." *O diário* 13 Março: 4-5.

Lívio, Tito. 1987. "'Montedemo.' A Dimensão do Fantástico." *A Capital* 15 de Setembro: 33.

Lourenço, Eduardo. 1984. "Literatura e Revolução." *Colóquio/Letras* Março: 7-16.

Louro, Regina. 1983. "A surpresa no feminino." *Expresso* 5 Fevereiro: 26-7.

——. 1984. Interview. "Lídia Jorge: 'Este terceiro livro é o primeiro'." *Jornal de Letras* 18-24 de Dezembro: 2-3.

Macciocchi, Maria-Antonietta. 1976. "Sexualité féminine dans l'idéologie fasciste." Trans. Nicole Famà. *Tel Quel* 66: 26-42.

Magalhães, Isabel Allegro de. 1987. *O Tempo das Mulheres.* Lisboa: Imprensa Nacional: Casa da Moeda.

——. 1995. *O Sexo dos Textos e Outras Leituras.* Lisboa: Caminho.

Mailer, Phil. 1977. *Portugal: The Impossible Revolution?* London: Solidarity.

Martins, Luís Almeida. 1988. "Lídia Jorge, Notícia do cais dos prodígios." *Jornal de Letras* 15-22 de Fevereiro: 6-10.

Medeiros, Paulo de. 1993. "O som dos búzios: feminismo, pós-modernismo, simulação." *Discursos Femininos.* Special issue of *Discursos. Estudos de Língua e Cultura Portuguesa* 5: 29-47.

Melo, Rose Nery Nobre de. 1975. *Mulheres Portuguesas na Resistência.* Lisboa: Seara Nova.

Metrass, Célia, Helena de Sá Medeiros and Maria Teresa Horta. 1975. *Aborto – Direito ao Nosso Corpo.* Lisboa: Futura.

Moi, Toril, ed. and intro. 1986. *The Kristeva Reader.* Oxford: Blackwell.

Moore-Gilbert, Bart. 1997. *Postcolonial Theory, Contexts, Practices, Politics.* London and New York: Verso.

Morão, Paula. 1988. Review of *Sara*, by Olga Gonçalves. *Colóquio/Letras* Janeiro-Fevereiro: 122-3.

Moreiras, Alberto. 1996. "The Aura of Testimonio." *The Real Thing. Testimonial Discourse and Latin America.* Ed. Georg M. Gugelberger. Durham and London: Duke University Press. 192-224.

Morgan, Robin. 1978. "International Feminism. A Call for Support of the Three Marias." *Going too Far. The Personal Chronicle of a Feminist.* New York: Vintage Books. 201-8.

——. 1996a. "Portugal." Morgan, *Sisterhood* 567-71.

——. ed. 1996b. *Sisterhood is Global. The International Women's Movement Anthology.* New York: The Feminist Press at the City University of New York.

Movimento de Libertação das Mulheres. n.d. "sobre o feminismo." Unpublished manifesto. MLM file. Comissão para a Igualdade e para os Direitos das Mulheres, Lisbon. 3.

Mulheres Contra Homens? 1971. Lisboa: Cadernos Dom Quixote.

Nunes, Maria Luísa. 1987. "Portuguese Women and Decolonization." *Becoming True to Ourselves. Cultural Decolonization and National Identity in the Literature of the Portuguese-Speaking World.* Contributions to the Study of World Literature 22. New York and Westport: Greenwood Press.

O'Malley, Mary. 1997. *The Knife in the Wave.* Cliffs of Moher: Salmon.

Organização das Mulheres Comunistas. 1994. *Subsídios para a História das Lutas e Movimentos de Mulheres em Portugal sob o Regime Fascista (1926-1974).* Lisboa: Edições Avante.

Ornelas, José. 1993. "Subversão da topografia cultural do patriarcado em *O Cavalo de Sol* de Teolinda Gersão." *Discursos Femininos.* Special issue of *Discursos. Estudos de Língua e Cultura Portuguesa* 5: 115-134.

Owen, Hilary. 1989. "The Three Marias: The case re-opened." *ACIS Journal* 2.1: 25-32.

——. 1992. "Feast or Faminism?: Women, Revolution and Class in Works by Hélia Correia and Olga Gonçalves." *Forum for Modern Language Studies* 27.4: 363-75.

——. 1995. "'Um quarto que seja seu': The Quest for Camões's Sister." *Portuguese Studies* 11: 179-91.

——. ed. and intro. 1996. *Gender, Ethnicity and Class in Modern Portuguese-Speaking Culture.* Lewiston, Queenston, Lampeter: Edwin Mellen Press.

——. 1999a "Back to Nietzsche: The Making of an Intellectual/Woman. Lídia Jorge's *A Costa dos Murmúrios.*" *Lídia Jorge. in other words/por outras palavras.* Ed. Cláudia Pazos Alonso. Special issue of *Portuguese Literary and Cultural Studies* 2: 79-98.

——. 1999b. "Exiled in its own Land." *Portugal the Last Empire.* Special Issue of *Index on Censorship* January: 57-60.

——. 1999c. "New Cartographies of the Body in *Novas Cartas Portuguesas.* The (Counter-) Narrative of the Nation and the Sign of the Voyage Back."

Engendering the Nation. Special issue of *Ellipsis. Journal of the American Portuguese Studies Association.* 1: 45-61.

Pazos Alonso, Cláudia. 1999a . "Repensar o feminino: O *Montedemo*, de Hélia Correia." *via atlântica* 2:109-119.

——. 1999b. "Sex and Success in *Notícia da Cidade Silvestre*: A Tale of Two Cities." *Lídia Jorge. in other words/por outras palavras.* Ed. Cláudia Pazos Alonso. Special issue of *Portuguese Literary and Cultural Studies* 2: 33-47.

Pazos Alonso, Cláudia with Glória Fernandes, eds. 1996. *Women, Literature and Culture in the Portuguese-Speaking World.* Lewiston, Queenston, Lampeter: Edwin Mellen Press.

Pedrosa, Inês. 1984. "Teolinda Gersão. 'Interessa-me captar o inconsciente em relâmpagos." *Jornal de Letras* 26 de Junho – 2 de Julho: 4.

Pimlott, Ben and Jean Seaton. 1983. "Political Power and the Portuguese Media." *In Search of Modern Portugal. The Revolution and its Consequences.* Ed. Lawrence S. Graham and Douglas L. Wheeler. Madison: The University of Wisconsin Press. 43-57.

Pintasilgo, Maria de Lourdes. 1980. Prefácio. *Novas Cartas Portuguesas.* By Maria Isabel Barreno, Maria Teresa Horta and Maria Velho da Costa. Lisboa: Moraes Editores. 11-28.

——. 1986. "Deambulação pelo Espaço/Tempo do 25 de Abril." *Revista Crítica de Ciências Sociais* Fevereiro: 63-70.

——. 1996. "Daring to be Different." Morgan, *Sisterhood is Global* 571-75.

Pinto, António Costa. 1992. "The New State of Salazar: An Overview." *The New Portugal: Democracy and Europe.* Ed. Richard Herr. Research Series Number 86. Berkeley: University of California at Berkeley International and Area Studies.

——. ed. 1998. *Modern Portugal.* Palo Alto: The Society for the Promotion of Science and Scholarship, Inc.

Pinto, Júlio. 1985. Interview with Lídia Jorge. *Diário de Notícias* 23 Junho: 4-6.

Prado Coelho, Eduardo. 1982. Review of *Paisagem com Mulher a Mar ao Fundo,* by Teolinda Gersão. *Jornal de Letras* 20 de Julho – 2 de Agosto: 21.

Pratt, Annis with Barbara White, Andrea Loewenstein and Mary Wyser. 1981. *Archetypal Patterns in Women's Fiction.* Brighton: Harvester Press.

Prewo, Dorotea. 1987. "'Ich bin fast erstickt'." *Frankfurter Rundschau* 1 September: 18-19.

Raby, D. L. 1988. *Fascism and resistance in Portugal. Communists, liberals and military dissidents in the opposition to Salazar, 1941-1974.* Manchester and New York: Manchester University Press.

Rodrigues, Urbano Tavares. 1986. "Loucura e fuga nas narrativas de Hélia Correia." *O diário* 26 Janeiro: 4.

Sadlier, J. Darlene. 1989. *The Question of How. Women Writers and New Portuguese Literature.* Contributions in Women's Studies 109. New York and Westport: Greenwood Press.

"Salazar e as Mulheres." 1977. *Opção* 17 de Agosto: 51-4.

Santos, Boaventura de Sousa. 1992. "11/1992. (Onzes Teses por Ocasião de Mais uma Descoberta de Portugal)." *Luso-Brazilian Review* 29.1: 97-113.

——. 1997. "State and Society in Portugal." Kaufman and Klobucka, *After the Revolution* 31-72.

Santos, Maria Irene Ramalho de Sousa and Ana Luísa Amaral. 1997. "Sobre a 'Escrita Feminina'." Centro de Estudos Sociais 90. Coimbra: Oficina da CES.

Sapega, Ellen. 1997. "No Longer Alone and Proud: Notes on the Rediscovery of the Nation in Contemporary Portuguese Fiction." Kaufman and Klobucka, *After the Revolution* 168-86.

Seixo, Maria Alzira. 1999. *"Novas Cartas Portuguesas. O Jogo das Damas." Jornal de Letras* 27 de Janeiro – 9 de Fevereiro: 20-21.

Silva, Regina Tavares da. 1982. *Feminismo em Portugal na voz de mulheres escritoras do início do séc. XX.* Lisboa: Comissão da Condição Feminina.

Silva-Brummel, Fernanda. 1993."Olga Gonçalves: Chronistin der portugiesischen Gegenwart." Engelmayer und Hess 119-39.

Simões, João Gaspar. 1985. "Os 'prodígios' de Lídia Jorge." *Diário de Notícias* 24 de Janeiro: 31.

Slover, Loretta Porto. 1977. "The Three Marias: Literary Portrayals of the Situation of Women in Portugal." Unpublished Dissertation. Harvard University.

Sousa, Antónia de. 1985. Interview with Lídia Jorge. "O êxito é uma roupa que tenho por vestir." *Diário de Notícias* 9 de Junho: 6.

——. 1998. Interview with Maria Isabel Barreno, Maria Teresa Horta and Maria Velho da Costa. *"Novas Cartas Portuguesas. 25 Anos Depois. Três Marias abalaram ditadura." Diário de Notícias* 7 de Novembro: 4-7.

Spivak, Gayatri. 1994. "Can the Subaltern Speak?" Ed. Patrick Williams and Laura Chrisman. *Colonial Discourse and Postcolonial Theory. A Reader.* New York: Colombia University Press. 66-111.

Teixeira, Nuno Severiano. 1998. "Between Africa and Europe: Portuguese Foreign Policy, 1890-1986." Pinto, *Modern Portugal* 60-87.

Vidal, Duarte. 1974. *O Processo das Três Marias. Defesa de Maria Isabel Barreno.* Lisboa: Futura.

Warner, Marina. 1990. *Alone of all her Sex. The myth and cult of the Virgin Mary.* London: Picador.

Young, Robert J. C. 1996. *Torn Halves. Political conflict in literary and cultural theory.* Manchester: Manchester University Press.

INDEX

WOMEN'S STUDIES

1. Nebraska Sociological Feminist Collective, **A Feminist Ethic for Social Science Research**

2. Mimi Scarf, **Battered Jewish Wives: Case Studies in the Response to Rage**

3. Sally-Ann Kitts, **The Debate on the Nature, Role and Influence of Woman in Eighteenth-Century Spain**

4. Kathryn N. Benzel and Lauren Pringle De La Vars (eds.), **Images of the Self as Female: The Achievement of Women Artists in Re-envisioning Feminine Identity**

5. Frances Richardson Keller (ed.), **Views of Women's Lives in Western Tradition: Frontiers of the Past and the Future**

6. James M. Boehnlein, **The Sociocognitive Rhetoric of Meridel Le Sueur: Feminist Discourse and Reportage of the Thirties**

7. Jesse W. Nash and Elizabeth Trinh Nguyen (eds.), **Romance, Gender, and Religion in a Vietnamese-American Community: Tales of God and Beautiful Women**

8. Mary V. Meckel, **A Sociological Analysis of the California Taxi-Dancer: The Hidden Halls**

9. Yvonne Day Merrill, **The Social Construction of Western Women's Rhetoric Before 1750**

10. Susan A. Lichtman, **The Female Hero in Women's Literature and Poetry**

11. Maria Manuel Lisboa, **Machado de Assis and Feminism: Re-reading the Heart of the Companion**

12. Jack George Thompson, **Women in Celtic Law and Culture**

13. Antonio Sobejano-Moran (ed.), **Feminism in Multi-Cultural Literature**

14. Helen Ralston, **The Lived Experience of South Asian Immigrant Women in Atlantic Canada: The Interconnections of Race, Class, and Gender**

15. Susanne Fendler (ed.), **Feminist Contributions to the Literary Canon: Setting Standards of Taste**

16. Dan Dervin, **Matricentric Narratives: Recent British Women's Fiction in a Postmodern Mode**

17. Deborah Burris-Kitchen, **Female Gang Participation: The Role of African-American Women in the Informal Drug Economy and Gang Activities**